what do we know and what should we do about...?

fake news

Nick Anstead

Los Angeles | London | New Delhi
Singapore | Washington DC | Melbourne

Los Angeles | London | New Delhi
Singapore | Washington DC | Melbourne

SAGE Publications Ltd
1 Oliver's Yard
55 City Road
London EC1Y 1SP

SAGE Publications Inc.
2455 Teller Road
Thousand Oaks, California 91320

SAGE Publications India Pvt Ltd
B 1/I 1 Mohan Cooperative Industrial Area
Mathura Road
New Delhi 110 044

SAGE Publications Asia-Pacific Pte Ltd
3 Church Street
#10-04 Samsung Hub
Singapore 049483

Editor: Natalie Aguilera
Editorial assistant: Esmé Carter
Production editor: Katherine Haw
Copyeditor: Neville Hankins
Proofreader: Clare Weaver
Marketing manager: George Kimble
Cover design: Lisa Harper-Wells
Typeset by: KnowledgeWorks Global Ltd.
Printed in the UK

Library of Congress Control Number:
2021932603

British Library Cataloguing in Publication data

A catalogue record for this book is available from the British Library

ISBN 978-1-5297-1789-1
ISBN 978-1-5297-1788-4 (pbk)

At SAGE we take sustainability seriously. Most of our products are printed in the UK using responsibly sourced papers and boards. When we print overseas we ensure sustainable papers are used as measured by the PREPS grading system. We undertake an annual audit to monitor our sustainability.

For my Dad, Nicholas John Anstead (1951–2020), with love.

contents

titles in the series

about the series

Every news bulletin carries stories which relate in some way to the social sciences – most obviously politics, economics and sociology, but also, often, anthropology, business studies, security studies, criminology, geography and many others.

Yet despite the existence of large numbers of academics who research these subjects, relatively little of their work is known to the general public.

There are many reasons for that, but, arguably, it is that the kinds of formats that social scientists publish in, and the way in which they write, are simply not accessible to the general public.

The guiding theme of this series is to provide a format and a way of writing which addresses this problem. Each book in the series is concerned with a topic of widespread public interest, and each is written in a way which is readily understandable to the general reader with no particular background knowledge.

The authors are academics with an established reputation and a track record of research in the relevant subject. They provide an overview of the research knowledge about the subject, whether this be long-established or reporting the most recent findings, widely accepted or still controversial. Often in public debate there is a demand for greater clarity about the facts, and that is one of the things the books in this series provide.

However, in social sciences, facts are often disputed and subject to different interpretations. They do not always, or even often, 'speak for themselves'. The authors therefore strive to show the different interpretations or the key controversies about their topics, but without getting bogged down in arcane academic arguments.

Not only can there be disputes about facts but also there are almost invariably different views on what should follow from these facts. And, in any case, public debate requires more of academics than just to report facts; it is also necessary to make suggestions and recommendations about the implications of these facts.

Thus each volume also contains ideas about 'what we should do' within each topic area. These are based upon the authors' knowledge of the field but also, inevitably, upon their own views, values and preferences. Readers may not agree with them, but the intention is to provoke thought and well-informed debate.

Chris Grey, Series Editor

Professor of Organization Studies

Royal Holloway, University of London

about the author

Nick Anstead is an Associate Professor in the Department of Media and Communications at the London School of Economics and Political Science. He was educated at Mansfield College, the University of Oxford, and Royal Holloway, the University of London, and previously was a lecturer in politics at the University of East Anglia. His research examines political communication, political institutions, democracy and public opinion. He tweets @nickanstead.

introduction

This short volume attempts to understand a term that has become ubiquitous in recent years: fake news. Whether we are talking about misinformation circulating during the 2016 US presidential election, the activities of the St Petersburg-based Internet Research Agency, or falsehoods targeting minority groups appearing on WhatsApp during elections in India, the world's largest democracy, talk of the challenge posed by fake news seems to be everywhere. The concept has generated much commentary, with academics producing books on the topic (Farkas & Schou, 2019; McNair, 2017) or related subjects such as post-truth politics (McIntyre, 2018), misinformation (O'Connor & Weatherall, 2019) and propaganda (Benkler, Faris, & Roberts, 2018). One respected BBC journalist even published a volume where he described society as having reached 'peak bullshit' (Davis, 2017).

However, ubiquity provides no guarantees of understanding or precision in a term's use, so it is certainly worth asking: what exactly do we mean by fake news, what do we know about it and what can we do about it?

This book addresses these questions over the next four chapters. The first offers an historical account of fake news. This is a necessary response to an observation that is frequently made in discussions about fake news – specifically, that lies have always been a part of politics. A logical extension of this position is that contemporary concerns about fake news are in some way overblown or exaggerated. Another version of this argument holds that contemporary fake news only differs from historical examples in the scale of its production and the velocity it circulates at.

The historical account I offer is a response to these challenges and starts to sketch out an argument which will run through this volume: that is, our ideas of both truthfulness and falsehood are inherently bound up in questions of power, trust and authority, and the institutions and people on which they are bestowed. Our ideas of what is true – and by implication what is false – are very different to those that people might have had in the past. We are currently witnessing a major shift in who is trusted to provide information and how it is received. It is this that creates many of the questions and problems that this book focuses on.

In the next chapter, we turn our attention to empirical questions. The first set of issues to be addressed are contextual. How do citizens get their news and how is this changing? As importantly, how do people relate to politics? Both of these factors provide the essential context for debating fake news. The chapter then moves on to empirical questions about fake news itself. Where does it come from and why is it created? How widespread is it and how does it spread? Among which people? And – perhaps most importantly of all – what impact does fake news have on wider political processes in democratic societies?

This chapter will conclude by addressing another important issue: what don't we know about fake news that we need to know? Contemporary discussions about fake news are often framed in the context of the changing ways in which citizens get information and particularly the emergence of online social media services, such as Facebook and Twitter. However, social networks of this kind present a big challenge to researchers and regulators, and a lot remains unknown.

The next chapter looks at possible solutions to the problem of fake news. I subdivide these solutions into two different types. First, I examine policy-based solutions. These involve people and institutions in the news process (journalists, social media sites, governments or regulators) acting in a different way or providing different sorts of content. This section includes a variety of solutions, including actions that can be taken by social media platforms and increasing government regulation.

While these solutions have some merit, the argument I offer is that (with the possible exception of improved media literacy) they can only provide a 'sticking plaster' for a much larger problem – that is, how citizens relate to and think about political institutions, including the media. I therefore also consider what I term discursive solutions. Essentially, these are different ways of thinking about political institutions, the democratic process and the challenge of fake news. Reinventing these ideas can open up new avenues and solutions.

I expand on this point in the final chapter of the book, offering a brief conclusion where I situate the problem of fake news in a broader institutional, social and democratic context. This final chapter also includes a short postscript, considering some of the arguments made in this book in the context of the COVID-19 pandemic. In many ways, this event highlights the broader trends and challenges on which this book focuses. It certainly shows that the quality of information citizens have access to and the levels of trust they have in that information can be a matter of life and death.

Before we go any further, though, one important question needs to be addressed in this introduction: what exactly is fake news?

The problem of defining fake news

The term fake news has been central to political discussion in recent years. But what exactly is fake news? On the face of it, fake news seems like a very easy concept to define – simply put, information that is not true but is shared as if it is.

However, such a definition could cover a huge range of different types of content, created for a variety of different purposes. One way to tackle this challenge is to create a typology of fake news. A prominent article on the subject undertook a literature review of academic research that used the term fake news to see how it had been employed (Tandoc, Lim, & Ling, 2018). This overview provided no fewer than six different types of fake news:

1. **Satire.** Defined as fake news because it adopted many of the presentational elements of real news communication. Focused on political events for humour.

2. **Parody.** Similar to satire, in that it adopted many of the presentational features of real news, but did not draw so heavily on real news content. Instead, it mocked the style of news coverage.

3. **Fabrication.** Made-up news stories, with the intention of misleading the audience (this is why it differs from parody).

4. **Photo manipulation.** This focuses on manipulation of visual items in news content.

5. **Propaganda.** Inaccurate content produced by governments to mislead or change the minds of either domestic or international audiences.

6. **Advertising and public relations.** Media that is created to look like news, but with the intention of selling a product to the public.

These definitions are further organized based on whether they intend to deceive viewers (news parody does not intend to deceive, propaganda does) and the extent to which different types of fake news rely on any kind of facts as the basis for their content (satire is a response to an established base of facts, fabrication is completely made up).

While useful in some situations, multi-faceted definitions of this kind can never be entirely satisfactory. At least some of the types overlap to some degree. Satire and parody seem very close to each other, for example. Furthermore, this sort of definition inevitably emphasizes what is different across the range of fake news described, rather than what is similar and unifies the concept. If we can identify six types of fake news, do we really have a definition at all?

There are other challenges in defining fake news. Definitions are hard to separate from the purposes they are being created for. Many computer scientists, for example, are interested in developing automated tools that can identify and filter untrue news stories. This sort of work requires a very clear definition that a computer is capable of applying. One article in the journal *Computer* suggests 'we skip the philosophical debates and deal with fake news at a technological level' (Berghel, 2017, p. 87).

Needless to say, social scientists take a very different approach. For them, fake news is a term to be studied in its wider context. Necessarily, this means fake news cannot be understood simply as a form of content, but rather as something that has a wider social existence. This approach was reflected in an article published in the journal *Nature* which was authored by a number of leading social scientists. The definition of fake news they offered was 'fabricated information that mimics news media content in form but not in organizational process or intent' (Lazer et al., 2018).

This deceptively simple definition contains no fewer than four elements:

1. **Fabricated:** the content is untrue.

2. **Genre/appearance:** the content is presented in a form that makes it look like genuine news media.

3. **Production:** the content is not created in the manner of traditional news.

4. **Purpose:** the intent of the content is not the same as traditional news.

The definition is further complicated by elements 3 and 4 being negative descriptions: that is, the production process and purpose are said to be *not* the same as traditional news, but there is no positive statement as to what the process or intent of fake news actually is (as discussed in the next chapter, fake news is created in a number of different ways for a variety of reasons).

Another definitional problem is that academics and policy-makers cannot really decide if fake news is a useful concept at all. This debate has become more prominent since populist politicians, notably Donald Trump, started talking about fake news as a way to attack media organizations whose coverage they dislike. This problem was highlighted by The House of Commons Digital, Culture, Media and Sport Committee in the UK who conducted a major investigation on the issue. In its final report, it declined to use the term fake news, as it had 'taken on a variety of meanings, including a description of any statement that is not liked or agreed with by the reader' (House of Commons Digital, Culture, Media and Sport Committee, 2019, p.10). Instead, the Committee followed a precedent set in recent academic work on the topic and opted for the twin terms of disinformation, which is inaccurate information created with the intention of causing harm or disruption, and misinformation, which is inaccurate information created without intent (for the original articulation of this distinction, see Wardle & Derakhshan, 2017).

The mis/disinformation dichotomy based on intent has proved popular. However, the focus on intent is problematic, for a couple of reasons. First, intent is a very difficult thing to measure. We cannot assume it simply from analyzing a piece of content published online. Second, how readers interpret a news story is not necessarily related to the intent of its creator.

A piece of satire might not appear misleading when published on an obviously humorous website. However, it could easily be reposted on social media and, stripped of context, become something that people actually believe.[1]

Towards an institutional definition of fake news

It will be unsurprising to readers that this volume contends that fake news is a useful concept. That said, it must be deployed with care in order to enhance rather than diminish our understanding. In order to offer a useful definition, it is worth first revisiting the way in which the term has historically been deployed in academic and public discourse.

Broadly speaking, the idea of fake news has been thought of in three different ways in the past two decades:

1. **Fake news as comedy.** Although not really the subject of this volume, fake news has a longer history than the contemporary interest in the topic. Particularly prior to the events of 2016, the term fake news was used to describe television programmes such as *The Daily Show* in the United States and *The Day Today* in the UK, or news websites such as *The Onion*. The unifying feature in these examples is that they consciously mocked the genre and presentation (and, on occasion, the pomposity) of the actual news for satirical effect.

2. **Fake news as misleading content.** The events of 2016 – notably the UK's decision to leave the European Union and Donald Trump's election – led to a new definition of fake news, which came to dominate not only academic discussion but also political, journalistic and popular discourse. I suspect it is this definition that most readers had in mind when they picked up this book. In this context, fake news simply meant fabricated stories that were circulating. To cite one seminal example, a story appeared during the 2016 US election claiming that Pope Francis had endorsed Donald Trump. This story led to 960,000 interactions on Facebook (i.e. people liking, sharing or commenting on the story) despite having no factual basis of any kind (Silverman, 2016b).

3. **Fake news as populist discourse.** The final definition turns the earlier iteration of fake news as misleading content on its head. Populist politicians in various countries have taken to using the term fake news

as a rhetorical device to attack media organizations they perceive to be their opponents. Investigative journalism which uncovers their campaign corruption or their administrative incompetence can thus quickly be dismissed as simply more 'fake news' produced by organizations with a political agenda.

Can these seemingly disparate and even outright contradictory versions of fake news be unified? One similarity between them is that they all in some respect reflect a broader institutional crisis within liberal democracies. While in retrospect the first generation of satirical fake news may seem benign (certainly in comparison with modern iterations of fake news), its purpose was to offer a critique of the contemporary political and journalistic class. Satirical fake news rose to prominence at a moment when the primary concern about democratic health was a generation of seemingly image-obsessed technocratic politicians and a parallel disengagement from democratic processes among citizens, especially young voters. Indeed, for a period of time there was hope that this sort of satirical fake news would actually prove beneficial to the relationship between citizens and democracy, increasing engagement with democratic institutions and levels of political knowledge among the public.[2] In this sense, and even if the satire was pretty vicious at times, its creators could still be seen as constructive critics of liberal democratic institutions.

Fake news as misleading content exploited the growing weakness of the same political and media institutions. This weakness was partly a question of decreasing dominance of traditionally powerful media organizations. People could potentially get their news from a much wider range of sources than was previously the case. They also tended to trust traditional news producers less than they historically had. At the same time, long-established conduits for political participation were suffering from declining trust and participation. Fewer people were members of political parties, for example. Across most democracies, citizens had a more negative view of the political class generally. This vacuum was filled with new ways of creating and sharing information, particularly online. At the same time, novel forms of political organization and models of organizing emerged. This is a complex process with a variety of consequences, but one important outcome was that a small political and journalistic elite lost much of its ability to act as gatekeepers, shaping the boundaries of public discourse. In this new environment, political debates have simultaneously become more porous and more fragmented, leaving the way open for more viewpoints and information to circulate, including fake news (these processes are discussed in more depth in Chapter 3).

Finally, fake news as populist rhetoric can be understood as representing a full-frontal assault on democratic and particularly journalistic institutions. Even before his inauguration, Donald Trump attacked CNN for publishing a story about Russian involvement in the 2016 presidential election. Trump refused to take a question from a reporter from the network in a press conference, on the grounds that 'you're fake news' (Jamieson, 2017). The Trumpian mangling of syntax is unsurprising, but also revealing of this particular iteration of fake news. The 'you're' is indicative that this version of fake news is directed not at content (i.e. an untrue story) but instead at an individual journalist or the institution they work for. In an environment where these institutions are already struggling for legitimacy, this form of attack is a powerful rhetorical device.

Therefore, what links the three forms of fake news – fake news as satire, fake news as misleading content and fake news as populist rhetoric – is they represent distinct responses to an ongoing and evolving crisis in democratic and media legitimacy.

This definition has important consequences for understanding the challenge of fake news. First, contemporary discussions of fake news cannot be decoupled from the specific historic moment we are living through. Second, and while political lying takes place in all types of regimes, whether democratic or authoritarian, this particular form of fake news exists in societies with democratic institutions.

Third, this leads to an uncomfortable and seemingly paradoxical truth: fake news is simultaneously of democratic life and also profoundly anti-democratic.[3] It is the product of the inherently competitive and open nature of democratic politics, where competing politicians and campaigns seek to assert their views and opinions, and use claim and counterclaim to undermine their opponents. At the same time, fake news challenges and undercuts certain ideas central to democracy. It prevents citizens from arriving at informed choices based on reliable information (although, as discussed in Chapter 3, it is questionable whether citizens actually engage with politics in such a rational manner). Furthermore, fake news can be used to launch attacks against institutions that are central to liberal democratic life – a free press, election regulators or an independent judiciary, for example – and undermine public confidence in these institutions.

Fake news can also be used to victimize specific individuals or groups in society in a way that is incompatible with the promise of equality that exists within democratic politics.

It is this Janus-faced aspect that makes fake news a much bigger challenge than it might first appear. It is not just a case of removing some untrue content or policing social media sites. Rather, it is a question of building institutions that are more robust and enjoy enough public confidence in a rapidly evolving and unpredictable political and information environment.

Notes

1. Academic research suggests this is surprisingly common. One American study found that a substantial number of citizens believed satirical news stories to be true. Levels of belief tended to follow partisan lines, with conservatives more likely to believe right-wing satirical websites, and liberals more likely to believe left-wing satirical websites (Garrett, Bond, & Poulsen, 2019).
2. This hope did not quite match up with the evidence. Generally, those who consumed political satire of this kind already had high levels of knowledge of and engagement with the political system (Young & Tisinger, 2006).
3. This argument echoes Krekó and Enyedi (2018) who argue that Viktor Orbán's political success in Hungary cannot be understood outside the context of competitive democratic politics, even while his party Fidesz uses power to attack the institutions and undermine the norms of democratic life. The example of Hungary is also a useful reminder that, for many parts of the world, fake news was a problem long before 2016.

2

background

Intentionally produced and shared disinformation is certainly nothing new. It is as old as politics itself. And so, the argument continues, if fake news has always been with us, maybe there is an over-reaction to the current situation?

The history offered below is by no means exhaustive. We could go back even further in time. Gossip was a central part of the politics of ancient Greek city states. There are a number of reasons for this. Many of the city states – notably Athens, Corinth and Syracuse – had democratic models of government, which made public opinion and popular decision-making central to politics. Additionally, Greek politics was highly personalized, with decisions often being made based on the characteristics of an individual citizen. In such an environment, it is hardly surprising that rumours spread swiftly and gained political significance, nor is it unexpected that some of these stories were false and deliberately circulated to undermine political opponents (McHardy, 2020).

Libellous stories played a part in some of the most seismic events in Roman history too. Following the assassination of Julius Caesar, his adopted son Octavian claimed that his rival for power, Mark Antony, was a would-be dictator who would destroy the Roman Republic. Evidence for this was provided by Mark Antony's affair with Cleopatra, and a suggestion he had developed autocratic tendencies while in Egypt. Octavian defeated Mark Antony at the Battle of Actium in 31 BC, consolidating his grip on power. Then, proving that political hypocrisy is as old as political disinformation, he abolished the Republic and transformed himself into Augustus Caesar, the first Roman Emperor (Kaminska, 2017).

However, we start our history of information, truth and falsity in the medieval world. The examples chosen often share characteristics with contemporary fake news, and historically recurring patterns are highlighted. What is important, though, is that these earlier iterations of disinformation are distinctive from the current predicament because the societies they occurred in had a very different understanding of the construction of truth and falsity. The idea of truth, how it is revealed and who has the authority to reveal it will vary greatly from society to society, and across history. Therefore, we cannot separate issues of falsity and truthfulness from questions of authority, trust and power, and the institutional setting in which they are bestowed.

Controlling the truth in medieval Europe

Medieval chroniclers are some of the most important sources we have for a period that would otherwise be lost to us. However, we have to handle their accounts with care: many chroniclers were highly partisan, acting as propagandists for particular political leaders. Others wrote with the aim of publicizing religious cults focused on specific saints, or with the intention of attacking other religious groups.

One such example is *The Life and Miracles of St William of Norwich* which appeared in 1172 and was written by Thomas of Monmouth. The book details the disappearance and death of the 12-year-old William in Norwich, providing 'evidence' (based on testimony given by surviving witnesses to Thomas several decades after the events in question) that he was crucified by the city's Jews before Easter, 1144. The reason for this crime, Thomas argues, is that the Jews in Norwich were part of a wider European network who believed that the sacrifice of Christian children would ensure their return to the Holy Land. Thomas then goes on to detail several miracles attributed to William since his death (Rose, 2015).

There are a number of similarities between *The Life and Miracles of St William of Norwich* and contemporary examples of fake news. First, the motivation may have been as much financial as theological. A successful saint's cult could be very lucrative for the local church because it attracted pilgrims. Certainly, there is some evidence that Thomas's writing was encouraged by Norwich's religious authorities. Second, the idea of a Jewish blood libel 'went viral' across medieval England and Europe. In the decades that followed, similar stories of child sacrifice emerged in a variety of cities, including Baden, Bern, Blois, Bury, Gloucester, Lincoln and Weissenberg.

The third trait recognizable from contemporary fake news is the singling out of minority groups as a target for attack. Indeed, one eminent historian of the period has argued that Thomas's fabrications are the starting point for modern anti-Semitism (McCulloh, 1997). Rumours about blood libel undermined the position of England's Jews in the following decades. This culminated in their expulsion by Edward I in 1290. Similar anti-Semitic canards have echoed down the centuries, including the infamous early twentieth-century hoax *The Protocols of the Elders of Zion*, which purported to document a conspiracy for Jewish world domination. Despite being completely debunked as a fake in the 1920s, *The Protocols* became central to the ideology of Nazi Germany and is still commonly cited by contemporary far-right groups.

Thomas of Monmouth's combination of fabrication, virulent anti-Semitism and shameless commercialism (in the hope of making a quick buck for the medieval Norwich tourist industry) make him a particularly unappealing historical figure. Not all chroniclers in the Middle Ages had Thomas's blasé attitude to factual accuracy. However, nor should the practices of even the most diligent chronicler be confused with the work of modern historians or journalists.

For medieval chroniclers, truth was inherently bound up in religious belief, and was essentially a moral and theological idea. If one reads various medieval accounts of battles, a pattern soon begins to emerge: the winning side were always pious, while the losing side were sinful and ill-disciplined. It seems a stretch to imagine these accounts were always accurate but that does not mean, for those who wrote them, they were not truthful. Instead, they revealed an underlying truth about the world – specifically, that the Godly would prevail and the immoral would be vanquished (Given-Wilson, 2004).

The medieval idea of truth is most obviously visible in the Bible. This led to conflict in the latter part of the Middle Ages over who would have access to the text and in which language. Even before the advent of printing, this period saw various efforts to translate the Bible into vernacular languages. In turn, the Church aggressively responded to these translations, often persecuting those involved as heretics.

The problem, as viewed from the perspective of the Church's hierarchy, was that once you gave people access to the words of the Bible in their own language, the clergy would lose their control over how those words were interpreted. This would lead to (in the view of the established Church) false deviation from orthodox religious doctrine, with unpredictable theological and political consequences. This concern was not unfounded. Dissident Oxford academic John Wycliffe completed his English translation of the Bible in 1382. Wycliffe and his followers, known as the Lollards, also critiqued the doctrine of transubstantiation, denied the special status of the priesthood (allowing women to preach) and attacked the Catholic Church for corruption (Aston, 1980; Rex, 2002).

The role of biblical interpretation was not limited to the spiritual arena, however. In a society where religion was so central to both daily life and legitimating authority, it was inevitable that these ideas would cross over into politics. Heretical ideas were linked to civil unrest, most famously expressed in the speech by the lay preacher John Ball on Blackheath during the Peasants' Revolt in 1381:

> When Adam delved and Eve span, Who was then the gentleman? From the beginning all men by nature were created alike, and our bondage or servitude came in by the unjust oppression of naughty men... And therefore I exhort you to consider that now the time is come, appointed to us by God, in which ye may (if ye will) cast off the yoke of bondage, and recover liberty. (Quoted in Dobson, 1983)

Here then was the proof: if the masses were allowed to read and interpret biblical texts for themselves, they would develop radical and dangerous ideas which had the potential to challenge the very foundations and the hierarchy on which medieval society was constructed. Unsurprisingly, at this point, the state's response to Lollardism and other deviations from Church orthodoxy intensified. After the Peasants' Revolt was quelled, Ball was hung, drawn and quartered, and his head displayed on a pike. In 1382, the Church held a synod which judged many of Wycliffe's ideas as heretical. While Wycliffe died of natural causes in 1384, his writings were also declared heretical in 1415 and his books burnt. Additionally, for good measure, his body was dug up and burnt in 1428. Many of Wycliffe's followers were not so lucky, suffering the same fate, but as a means of execution.

However, the story of Lollardism is more complex than a small religious sect that challenged authority and was subsequently crushed by the state and the Church. Lollards were not without powerful supporters. Wycliffe and early Lollards were offered some protection by John of Gaunt, the son of Edward III and the leading political figure in the country during the minority of Richard II. While John's support for Lollardy waned as the sect became more radical, his relationship with the group is a reminder that anti-elite movements frequently have friends in high places and can often also be understood as being actors in intra-elite conflict. John of Gaunt, it has been suggested, saw Wycliffe as a counterbalance to powerful Church interests who opposed him politically (Rex, 2002, pp. 28–29).

Additionally, the example of Lollardy and other heretical sects from this period show that the connection between conflicts over information and the way it is controlled can never be separated from a wider social context. Lollardy and other heresies emerged, grew and were repressed at a time that historians have called the late medieval crisis (Bois, 1998). This Europe-wide phenomenon was triggered by a number of interconnected events, including famines in the early fourteenth century and continuing wars between major powers, notably the Hundred Years War between England and France. However, the most significant cause of the crisis was the Black Death, which arrived in Europe in the late 1340s. While estimates vary, the plague likely killed at least a third of the population of the continent, and considerably larger proportions in some locations. A cataclysm on this scale led to the emergence of a variety of radical and violent responses, from cults based on self-flagellation to anti-Semitic pogroms (Ziegler, 2013).

The shortage of labour created by such high death rates undermined feudalism, the economic arrangement on which medieval societies were based. In a feudal system, peasants were bound to their lords, exchanging labour for a small area of land which allowed them to live a subsistence existence. However, following the ravishes of the Black Death, the Peasantry started to realize that their labour was now worth more on the open market. This realization created huge political and social instability across Europe, as the Peasantry attempted to extricate itself from the bondage of feudal serfdom. It was this tension that led to the Peasants' Revolt, and it was this context that framed debates over access to scripture. The social structures that had legitimized the institutions that had previously acted as the guardians of biblical truth came under attack, and new forms of access to (notably vernacular Bibles) and more radical interpretations of scripture emerged as a direct challenge to this authority.

Printing and literacy

Wycliffe has been called the morning star of the Reformation, a precursor to later Protestant thinkers. Certainly, later deviations from Catholic orthodoxy had a major advantage over their predecessors, as they had access to the printing press.

Europeans did not invent printing. China had used woodblock printing for centuries. Korea developed a technology very similar to movable type just before its appearance in Western Europe. However, it is in Western Europe that the idea of the printing press and the social changes it bought about dominates the historical imagination. The argument is most clearly articulated by the historian Elizabeth Eisenstein in her classic history of printing in Western Europe (1980). Eisenstein argues that the centrality of the printing press and what she terms the printing revolution has received insufficient attention from historians. Printing was pivotal to the development of three major intellectual movements in the centuries that followed. The Renaissance, which rediscovered the achievements of classic antiquity; the Reformation, which challenged the authority of the Catholic Church and divided Western Christendom; and the Enlightenment, with its commitment to reason and individual liberty. Without printing, Eisenstein argues, these intellectual movements could have easily fizzled out, instead of becoming seminal events in European and global history. Instead, printing actively encouraged the airing of mutually exclusive ideas and arguments, and in so doing undermined the power of institutions that tried to propagate a single truth.

Eistenstein's account is magisterial, but we should be wary of such grand narratives. While the development of printing clearly was a hugely significant event, it would be wrong to portray its impact as inevitable or predetermined. Rather, the consequences of printing were diverse and unpredictable, varying greatly from place to place. In some parts of Europe, printing actually strengthened the Church's control over scripture, because the errors that had inevitably crept into documents produced by scribes could now be identified and removed.

The primacy given to printing as a cause of social change is also problematic. In the nearly three centuries that Eisenstein surveys, vast economic, social, political and philosophical developments had occurred. Printing was certainly a significant part of these processes, but it existed within and interacted with a much wider network of developments.

For a truly mass audience to emerge for printed material, a second trend was required: increased literacy. It is very hard to estimate literacy levels in the past. Economic historian Bob Allen argued that literacy in various Western and Central European countries was 10 per cent or lower in 1500. This literate group would have been largely made up of clergy and a small professional and business elite. By 1800, Northern Europe had leapt ahead in literacy levels. The Netherlands had literacy rates of 68 per cent, England 53 per cent and Belgium 49 per cent. Allen argues that this growth was largely a product of increasing levels of economic prosperity in these societies. France and (the area that would become) Germany were slightly behind, at 37 per cent and 35 per cent respectively. Southern and Central European countries had lower literacy levels, generally around 20 per cent (Allen, 2003, p. 415).

The combination of printing and increasing literacy levels led to the emergence of what historians have called print culture. Printing became a highly profitable and rapidly expanding business. It has been estimated that the single year of 1550 saw the production of more than 3 million books. This is more volumes than were produced in the whole of the fourteenth century. The trend towards increased production continued into the eighteenth century. In the period between 1751 and 1800, for example, the Netherlands (the leading European consumer of books) was producing nearly one book for every two members of its population per annum (Buringh & Van Zanden, 2009). The same period saw the emergence of new genres of printed material, including the longform novel and the newspaper.

It is the German philosopher and sociologist Jürgen Habermas who perhaps best captures the vibrancy of print culture in *The Structural Transformation of the Public Sphere* (Habermas, 1989). Habermas argues that the late seventeenth century in England (and subsequently in Germany, France and the United States) saw the emergence of a literate and politically aware bourgeoise class. This group created a public sphere – a space that was neither under the control of government, nor private and domestic. The most famous manifestation of such a space is the coffee house, which provided a place to meet, read and engage in what Habermas termed rational-critical debate.

Habermas's theories have been both far-reaching and controversial. The sort of discussions occurring in the coffee house public sphere are a precursor to contemporary theories about deliberative democracy, where citizens rationally engage in debate, develop their opinions in response to new information and arrive at consensus opinions. Habermas has been critiqued for failing to recognize that the public sphere as he defines it is inherently unequal. To enter it, individuals need to have the sort of education that allows them to engage in debate with other citizens as peers. This, however, may exclude whole sections of a society. More broadly, there is the question about whether the type of rational, consensus-building debate that Habermasian theory espouses is a desirable way to conduct politics. It, for example, leaves little role for emotion in political discourse, nor does it recognize that some questions in politics may be inherently conflictual, as they are based on irreconcilable structural divisions (e.g. issues related to class, race or gender).

That said, Habermas's theory still provides an ideal (some might argue idealized) view of what liberal and rational debate should look like. If we want to understand the dismay at the emergence of fake news and the way in which political debate has developed in recent years, we would do well to think about how far removed they are from his model.

The development of the modern news industry and journalism

Habermas argued that the bourgeoise public sphere lasted for about a century and a half before going into decline. Key to this change was the rise of consumer capitalism, which started to permeate and pervert the public sphere. Nowhere was this development more obvious than the emergence of the mass publication newspaper industry.

This development was fuelled by a number of changes that occurred in the nineteenth century. Printing technology continued to evolve, making copies of texts ever quicker and cheaper to produce. At the end of the eighteenth century, printing presses could produce about 200 impressions per hour. The Applegate press, which was displayed at the Great Exhibition in 1851, was capable of producing 20,000 impressions per hour (Taunton, 2014). The audience for newspapers also continued to expand, with increased rates of literacy across the industrialized world (Lloyd, 2007). The business model of newspaper production changed as well.

Newspapers provided the perfect conduit for advertisers to communicate with increasingly affluent middle- and working-class consumers. In short, it was boom time for the newspaper industry.

It was this period that saw the media phenomenon that is most frequently drawn on when historical comparisons to fake news are sought. This is the tabloid publications known as the yellow press, which appeared in the United States in the late nineteenth century.

The rise of the yellow press was fuelled by the rivalry between Joseph Pulitzer and William Randolph Hurst, the owners of the *New York World* and *New York Journal* respectively. These newspapers invented much of what we would recognize today as the constituent elements of popular journalism: news was covered in a sensationalized and salacious manner, with a heavy focus on scandal and corruption; headlines were in large print and ran across the whole page, instead of just columns as had previously been the practice; sections of newspapers were specifically aimed at women or covered sports; photographs started to play a much more prominent role in layout; and cartoon strips became hugely popular.

There are certainly strong echoes in the reaction to the yellow press with contemporary concerns about fake news. As one modern commentator notes: 'Elite papers joined with upper-class magazines, reforming social scientists, and political leaders in criticizing the yellow press' (Kaplan, 2008, p. 2). Arguably this alliance would be a fairly accurate description of those most concerned about fake news today. Was the concern of the 1890s justified?

The most significant charge against the yellow press related to the 1898 Spanish–American war. The war started when Spain aggressively repressed a rebellion against its colonial rule of Cuba, just 90 miles (145 km) from the US mainland. This in turn triggered a negative response from both American political leaders and the mass media, including strongly anti-Spanish headlines in the yellow press in New York. President McKinley dispatched the battleship USS *Maine* to Cuba, nominally to protect US citizens on the island, but in reality as part of a wider set of naval manoeuvres designed to assert American dominance in the Caribbean. However, the situation escalated dramatically when the *Maine* was sunk in Havana harbour due to an unexplained explosion on 15 February 1898.

The cause of this explosion remains unclear. However, this did not stop the yellow press reporting Spanish involvement in the sinking as if it were a confirmed fact, attempting to whip up jingoism and pro-war feeling among the populace. By late April, Spain and the United States were at war. Historians writing in the decades after the event placed a significant portion of the blame for the conflict on the media. For example, Wilkerson argues that the yellow press was the primary cause of the war, as it had inflamed American public opinion against the Spanish (1932).

Modern scholarship has been far more sceptical about the actual effect of the yellow press in causing the war. Certainly, it was the case that sensationalist and untrue accounts of Spanish crimes against Cubans were being circulated in the yellow press, as were claims about Spanish involvement in the sinking of the *Maine* with no caveats expressing uncertainty or alternative theories. At the same time, though, it should be remembered that the yellow press was located in New York. It did not have the ability to shape nationwide public opinion. The Spanish–American War had a variety of causes, most significantly the changing power balance in the Caribbean, as American power increased and Spanish power receded. That said, it has also more recently been argued that the yellow press still acted as an enabler for war, helping to build a political environment where the conflict could occur (Hamilton, Coleman, Grable, & Cole, 2006).

The story of the yellow press has a wonderfully ironic conclusion. When Joseph Pulitzer died, he left two significant bequests: one to create the Columbia Journalism School and another to set up the eponymous prize, which has become a byword for journalistic quality, integrity and achievement.

Pulitzer's bequests highlight the changing nature of American journalism at the start of the twentieth century. As well as being part of a highly profitable industry, the role of the journalist was becoming increasingly professionalized and institutionalized. Professionalization was the product not just of formal education in journalism offered by institutions like Columbia, but also the development of a set of professional values. The exact form that these values took varied slightly across countries (Hallin & Mancini, 2004). In the United States, for example, a form of journalism emerged which claimed to be objective, and have a social function of investigating and holding accountable those in positions of authority.

What do we mean by objective journalism? The American media scholar Michael Schudson says:

Objective reporting is supposed to be cool, rather than emotional, in tone. Objective reporting takes pains to represent fairly each leading side in a political controversy. According to the objectivity norm, the journalist's job consists of reporting something called 'news' without commenting on it, slanting it, or shaping its formulation in any way. (2001)

For Schudson, objective journalism is the opposite of partisan journalism. Why did this journalistic norm emerge at this point in history in the United States? A number of explanations have been advanced. One argument is technological. The advent of the telegraph meant that information could now be communicated from a great distance very rapidly. However, it was a limitation of this form of communication that messages had to be expressed in a succinct style which suited the terse transmission of factual information. Another theory is that newspaper owners, increasingly mindful of their business model, moved away from partisan politics in order not to alienate potential readers. Schudson offers an alternative argument: that the turn to objectivity was a method for journalists to construct their professional identity, as distinct from the public relations and advertising experts who were also emerging at this time. The development of professional practices changed the way that journalists went about their day-to-day work. Note taking became common practice. So too did interviewing and quoting individuals who appeared in the stories covered. These were literary devices that demonstrated accuracy and objectivity (Schudson, 2001). Even though European countries did not adopt the American idea of objectivity to the same degree (British newspapers certainly do not claim to be non-partisan to anywhere near the same degree, for example), many of the same practices and writing techniques did cross the Atlantic.

Propaganda in the twentieth century

In much the same way as the First World War was the first industrialized conflict, it was also the first struggle fought through mass media. It saw all sides engaging in propaganda, both to mobilize their own citizens and to demonize their enemies. Allegations of German atrocities in Belgium were used to encourage recruitment in Britain and later the United States. The truth of the accusations against the invading German forces has been a subject of debate among historians for a century (on this see Zuckerman, 2004). However, what is beyond doubt is that the posters and news stories on the rape of Belgium were incredibly effective in whipping up anti-German feeling among civilians in Allied countries. First World War propaganda was effective because it combined new techniques developed in advertising, the capabilities of mass media, and the increased power of government. Additionally, it drew on a newly emerging popular national sentiment that had been forged in the nineteenth century (Anderson, 1983).

While propaganda was certainly used by both democracies and authoritarian states in the First World War, it was in the middle years of the twentieth century in totalitarian states that these techniques were refined to their most extreme and potent form. One only needs to look at an archive of Nazi or Soviet propaganda to see how vicious this material was, especially when directed at ideological opponents with the aim of dehumanizing them.

However, we would be somewhat missing the point if we only considered the posters and films made by these regimes, repellent though they are. Their propaganda was about more than selling citizens a set of lies. Rather, it was part of a broader attempt to construct an alternative reality. The scholar Federico Finchelstein (2020) argues that this idea is central to fascist ideology, which must at least in part be understood as a political project to redefine what the truth is. Fascism rejects verifiable reality and instead draws on its ideology and leader as the basis for constructing a new way of understanding the world. Essentially, the malevolent political and ideological fantasies of the party forge a new reality, to be promulgated and aggressively defended. Furthermore, if the idealized fascist reality clearly does not exist, then political will (including violence) must be used to conjure it into being.

It is easy to see why this approach proved so powerful, both in Fascist states in mid-twentieth-century Europe and in the communist states that existed at the same time. The capacity of these regimes to manage information and news media was great. They controlled film production and the radio, could censor newspapers, wrote school textbooks, forcibly closed down media institutions that opposed or were critical of them, and could make their political opponents disappear. In such a setting, regimes could go beyond simply telling distinct lies and instead promulgate whole ideological systems, be it the infallibility of the leader or Nazi Germany's anti-Semitic conspiracy theories.

However, it would be wrong to assume that citizens meekly accepted these messages as the unvarnished truth. During the Second World War, for example, plenty of Germans tuned into the BBC to get an alternative perspective on how the war was going (Doward, 2017). Another avenue for opposing the regime's version of the truth was humour. Jokes circulated that mocked the pomposity of the dictatorship or alluded to alternative truths that contradicted state propaganda. The regime recognized this challenge to its authority. German citizens were executed after being overheard telling anti-Nazi jokes (Crossland, 2006).

The example of Fascism might be comforting to us when we consider contemporary questions related to fake news. Even if we live in a time where fake news is in wide circulation, we also live at a moment where information is abundant and pluralistic. News stories can be checked, if we choose to do so. However, a more sober reading of the situation would be that our idea of truth is once again under attack from radical ideological movements, and this is a precursor to an alternative and recognizably fascist form of truth (Snyder, 2017, pp. 65–69).

It is because of this history that the word propaganda has such a bad reputation. In recent decades, countries have practised what has become known as public diplomacy. This was a term used during the Cold War to describe American communication efforts across the Iron Curtain, such as Radio Free Europe. It is debated among scholars in the field whether propaganda and public diplomacy actually amount to the same thing, but one argument made by practitioners of the latter is that there has to be at least a basis of truth in the information that is being shared for it to be effective. Complete fabrications ultimately end up backfiring, because you lose the trust of your target audience (Nye, 2008).

One thing is certain: at the beginning of the twenty-first century, many countries are increasingly thinking about public diplomacy as an important arm of their international relations arsenal. As we shall see, the current crisis of fake news is at least in part driven by international politics and rivalry between states.

Conclusion: the lessons of history

Fake news, as defined in this book at least, is a problem specific to contemporary liberal democracies. However, the contours of the ongoing crisis are recognizable from previous conflicts over truthfulness and falsity in earlier periods of history, for at least two reasons. First, there are similarities in the types of falsehoods being spread (they may attack particular minority groups, for example) and the reasons that lies are told (the desired outcomes could be financial or political). Second, and more significantly, while the circumstances are different, the larger historical process is recognizable. Specifically, an established system for legitimating truth is coming under attack.

While the above is by no means an exhaustive account of the history of truthfulness and falsity (the examples are taken largely from Western history, for one thing), it illustrates some key lessons about the evolving ways people have got information, who has had the authority to share that information and how that authority has been contested. From this account, I would suggest we can draw four key lessons, which will be useful as we go on to build our understanding of contemporary fake news.

First, all societies have methods for defining truthfulness and falsehood. Furthermore, they have individuals and institutions who are assumed to be able to practise these methods effectively, whether they are medieval chroniclers and priests, Enlightenment philosophers, or contemporary journalists.

Second, these methods for defining the truth are built on a broader view of the world. In the medieval period, truth was seen as a moral position related to religious adherence. This was a more important element of truth than factual accuracy. Modern journalism has come to prioritize accuracy and objectivity in its version of the truth.

Third, technology can play a significant role in undermining and challenging pre-existing truth systems. However, it is also dangerous and overly simplistic to adopt a position of technological determinism. This is a problem that is evident in much modern discussion of fake news, where explanations have often focused on the affordances of social media platforms and ignored broader contextual issues. Instead, it is better to try to understand how technological developments interact with other factors.

Finally, and related to this, times of political, social and economic instability make it more likely that the authority of those who claim to have access to the truth will be questioned, and alternative accounts will emerge. While alternative methods of defining the truth are hard to imagine, we have seen at least one attempt to impose a new truth system – fascism – within living memory.

what do we know?

This chapter not only examines what we know about the fake news phenomenon (where it comes from, whether people believe it, etc.), but also situates that information in a broader media and political context. It is impossible to understand the debate about fake news and the concern it generates without also telling this wider story. The emergence of fake news and our reaction to it is symptomatic of a larger set of changes in media and politics, and how they relate to each other.

How is our media consumption changing?

It is very tempting to divide patterns of media consumptions into neatly chronological periods – 'the radio age', 'the television age' and 'the internet age', for example. While this risks oversimplification (inevitably, there are overlaps between these periods with some people consuming media in a new way and others still consuming in the old way), it is still substantively accurate to say we have moved from a time of mass media to an era of fragmented media.

The difference between our world of media consumption and the high point of the mass media era is nicely highlighted by the great television critic Clive James, who detailed his experience of writing for the British *Observer* newspaper in the early 1970s:

> I was inhabiting a strange, half-lit world in which nothing happened except watching television. Often I had two sets running at once.

Elsewhere on earth, they were inventing the VCR machine, but too late to help me out. Every night I watched everything that mattered, and a lot more that was not supposed to, on three channels, which eventually grew to four. (2017)

The mass media era was a time when media choice was very restricted, at least by the standards we are now used to. On television, the number of channels was restricted by bandwidth, which limited the available broadcast frequencies. Programmes had to be consumed at the time of broadcast. If two programmes clashed – short of the two-television solution used by James – then a choice had to be made about which channel to watch. The limited choice of channels and the need to watch at time of broadcast also meant very high potential audiences for individual programmes. Similarly, newspapers operated in a very different way from today's publications. While there might have been multiple editions published in a day and a greater range of titles available at different times (more evening editions, for example), these were based around fixed print deadlines. The content of the edition became set at the point it went to the printers.

Mass media of this kind gave television and newspaper editors tremendous control over the information that was in public circulation. Furthermore, when information was included for publication, it could rapidly be disseminated to a very large audience.

In place of mass media consumption, we now have a media environment with increased consumer choice over what we watch and read, and how, when and where we consume it. These changes have included the development of more powerful time-shifting technologies (first video cassette recorders, and then solid-state recorders and finally online catch-up services), as well as a growing range of media platforms. We have moved from having a handful of broadcast television channels to satellite and cable services that carry hundreds of channels. Even more dramatically, online broadcasting now makes the number of channels available practically unlimited, while on-demand services such as Netflix store huge repositories of archived programmes.

The growing number of channels and online services has led to a growing segmentation and specialization in broadcasting (ranging from channels focused exclusively on rolling news coverage, nature documentaries or cooking programmes, and even channels dedicated to a particular football club). We can consume media in different locations or while we are on the move too. No longer is television consumption an activity limited to watching a large electronic device in the corner of our living room. We can now watch on our phones, tablets and laptops while out and about.

Newspapers have changed dramatically too, with many established brands moving online. This has changed their news production process. Instead of the print schedules created by fixed editions of newspapers, many publications now practise an 'online first' policy, where new content will appear on their websites at any time of the day or night. Like television news channels, newspapers have essentially become rolling news environments, publishing stories as soon as they are able.

The trend towards fragmentation has only intensified with the development of social media. This has led to entirely new modes of communication. When an individual opens up their Facebook account, the information they see on their news feed will be selected and organized in a form that is unique to them. This process is governed by Facebook's algorithm, which relies on information that users give Facebook – who their friends are, where they live, are they married or single, gay or straight, what their political or religious beliefs are, which posts they have liked, etc. – to make predictions about the type of content they are most likely to engage with. It is no exaggeration to say that, in the age of social media, everyone will have their own personal media in a manner that has never previously been the case.

Social media has also allowed us to become content creators to an extent that would have been unthinkable in the past. The combination of easily accessible publishing technologies (e.g. blogs, wikis and social media services) and relatively cheap devices capable of creating content and publishing it (such as consumer laptops, tablets and phones with cameras) means that the barriers to sharing text, images or video (often referred to as user-generated content) have declined greatly.

The rise of user-generated content is not just limited to social media sites. Older media organizations have also embraced this development. Giving audiences a voice is not entirely new. Newspapers have long had letters pages where a (strictly limited and vetted) number of readers could engage with the content of the publication. Now the web facilitates virtually unlimited user comments 'below the line' (i.e. underneath the original published material). Between 2006 and 2016, for example, the *Guardian* newspaper published nearly 70 million user comments on its Comment is Free platform (Mansfield, 2016).

The combination of fragmentation and user-generated content has undermined the role of editors as traditionally understood, as the arbiters and organizers of information entering the public domain. The information environment is now considerably more porous, and the boundaries of 'acceptable' debate are much harder to police. It only takes a few imaginary historical counterfactuals to grasp the scale of this change. Would it, for example, have been possible to keep Franklin Roosevelt's disability a secret in the age of camera phones? Could Winston Churchill's heavy drinking and (later in his career) declining health have been kept from the public when political gossip circulates so freely on blogs and social media? Both men's personal circumstances were known about by contemporary journalists, but were rarely actually referenced in reporting about them.[1] It is interesting to think about how sustainable such a situation would be today.

As a result of these developments, the corporate media landscape has changed dramatically. Some older companies have reinvented themselves to provide significant online offerings (Disney or the *New York Times*, for example), as have public service broadcasters (the BBC now has a vast online footprint and a significant global corporate offshoot). Computer firms have diversified into both creating and selling content (Apple), while new firms have emerged to do the same (Netflix and Spotify). In contrast, some major news providers, particularly newspapers, have ceased to exist (in the United States, a number of major newspaper firms filed for bankruptcy following the 2008 financial crisis and many, many local newspapers around the world have also closed), or shifted to new publishing models such as freesheets or become online-only publications (the *Evening Standard* and the *Independent* in the UK respectively).

The growing transnationalism of media consumption means that news is not only available 24 hours a day, but from a wider variety of international sources. This change is illustrated through the examples of two wars in the Middle East, just slightly more than a decade apart. The 1991 Gulf War became known as the CNN war, as the American rolling news channel pioneered live coverage of the conflict. CNN, for example, carried press conferences by senior military figures (Zelizer, 1992). By the era of the 'war on terror' and particularly the war in Afghanistan that started in 2001 and the war in Iraq in 2003, it was the Qatari state-owned news broadcaster Al Jazeera that was providing the most groundbreaking coverage. Although originally broadcasting in Arabic, Al Jazeera also produced English-language content, which was available in much of Europe and North America.

Al Jazeera's coverage has at times been controversial, but it is undeniable that its success reflects a growing internationalism and pluralism available in news offerings. Indeed, this shift to a more pluralistic broadcast environment and move away from a Western monopoly on news broadcasting became known as the Al Jazeera effect (Seib, 2008). More concerningly, though, the growing proliferation of news channels has also led to the emergence of broadcasters which were barely concealed mouthpieces for authoritarian states. In 2019, the UK broadcasting regulator Ofcom fined *Russia Today* £200,000 for breaching impartiality rules, particularly in its coverage of the Salisbury attacks and the war in Syria (Ofcom, 2019).

The most dramatic corporate development has been the emergence of new firms that have rapidly grown to become among the largest companies in the world, fuelled by new business models built around types of targeted advertising facilitated by social media platforms and search engines. While they were only founded relatively recently, the companies behind these services are now some of the largest in the world. Google was founded in 1998. Currently its parent company, Alphabet, is the fifth-largest company in the world by market capitalization. Facebook was founded in 2004, and is currently the sixth-largest company in the world (all data from Statistica, 2020). With the introduction of these new and very powerful corporate behemoths, the media industry has undergone a disruption of historic proportions.

Where do we get our news from?

We only need to think about contemporary media consumption patterns for a moment to appreciate how far away we are from the era of mass media. News and political communication in the earlier period is easy to imagine with reference to a few emblematic examples. President Roosevelt's fireside chats were conducted directly from the Oval Office and beamed out across the country into the homes of depression era and wartime America. Similarly, the televised debate between Vice President Richard Nixon and Senator John F. Kennedy in the 1960 presidential elections has taken on mythological significance. Indeed, its significance is mythological in a very literal sense: the most widely known part of the story about the debate – that listeners on radio thought that Nixon had won the debate, while viewers on television gave it Kennedy – is likely to be untrue.[2] But it neatly symbolizes a shift to the age of television in politics, a time when mass media served up information, beamed directly into living rooms through the evening news bulletin.

In contrast, the multi-channel, social, user-generated and above all fragmented environment that now exists has dramatically changed how people get their political news or indeed whether they get political news at all. However, where once political news was a shared experience with large segments of the population consuming the same items at the same time, it has now become an individualized process, with citizens configuring their own consumption by choosing from a range of sources. At one end of the spectrum, a minority of people are hyper-engaged, with the ability to monitor events in real time as they occur by watching rolling news or reading live news blogs on newspaper websites. At the other end of the spectrum, the level of media choice allows some viewers to opt out of news consumption altogether (Strömbäck, Djerf-Pierre, & Shehata, 2013). It is important to recognize that the move to a more fragmented media has had some positive consequences. Some evidence suggests, for example, that women and minority groups believe the news is becoming more reliable (Laura, 2019).

How have all these changes shaped where people actually get their news from? We can find evidence to help us answer this question by looking at data gathered by The Reuters Institute of Journalism at Oxford University in its annual survey of news consumption. The most recent version of the exercise examined 40 countries.

The survey asks participants where they get their news from (respondents are able to list multiple sources). The results of the 2020 survey are shown in Table 1. Collectively, the data tells an interesting story: television remains a significant news source in almost all countries, although the figure ranges from 44 per cent of participants in Singapore to 78 per cent in Portugal. However, in every single country surveyed, online news consumption (in all its forms) matches or exceeds television news consumption. This is most clearly the case in Singapore (where online consumption eclipses television consumption by +43 percentage points), Mexico (+38 percentage points), Malaysia (+36 percentage points), Norway (+27 percentage points) and Greece (+25 percentage points). This contrasts with countries like Germany (where both television and online news are used by 70 percentage points of people) and Italy (only +1 percentage points more online news consumption).

Table 1 News consumption by source in 40 different countries

Region	Country	Television	Print	Online (all)	Social media
Europe	Austria	68	51	71	45
	Belgium	63	33	77	41
	Bulgaria	77	24	86	71
	Croatia	76	36	88	55
	Czech Republic	76	24	88	49
	Denmark	62	21	80	47
	Finland	64	37	88	43
	France	64	15	66	39
	Germany	70	33	70	37
	Greece	67	24	92	71
	Hungary	67	15	84	64
	Ireland	64	32	80	50
	Italy	73	22	74	50
	Netherlands	67	33	77	39
	Norway	61	25	88	52
	Poland	75	24	87	66
	Portugal	78	33	80	58
	Romania	76	15	83	60
	Slovakia	76	22	79	54
	Spain	63	34	79	56
	Sweden	64	28	84	50
	Switzerland	59	48	77	44
	Turkey	68	42	85	58
	United Kingdom	55	22	77	39
Americas	Argentina	67	23	86	71
	Brazil	66	23	87	67
	Canada	60	25	78	53
	Chile	66	24	86	73
	Mexico	48	26	86	70
	United States	59	20	72	48
Asia-Pacific	Australia	63	25	76	52
	Hong Kong	71	31	85	66
	Japan	60	27	62	25
	Malaysia	50	30	86	70

(Continued)

Table 1 (Continued)

Region	Country	Television	Print	Online (all)	Social media
	Philippines	66	22	85	68
	Singapore	44	29	87	63
	South Korea	63	18	83	44
	Taiwan	62	21	83	59
Africa	Kenya	74	47	90	77
	South Africa	68	37	90	73

Source: Reuters Institute (2020) Digital News Report

As a subset of online news consumption, social media news consumption also varies across countries. Interestingly, it is very high in African countries, with Kenya having the highest social media news consumption of anywhere surveyed (77 per cent of respondents claim to get news from social media, compared with 74 per cent who use television) and South Africa the joint second-highest level (73 per cent social media news consumption). Chile (73 per cent), Bulgaria, Argentina and Greece (all 71 per cent) also feature highly on this list. At the other end of the spectrum, Japan has the lowest social media news consumption among the surveyed countries, although even there 25 per cent of citizens get news from social media. Other low-ranking countries in this metric include Germany (37 per cent), the UK, France and the Netherlands (all 39 per cent).

The final part of the media system covered in this survey is print. Austria (51 per cent of those surveyed got news from newspapers) and Switzerland (48 per cent) seem to have the strongest newspaper industries in terms of consumption. Interestingly, Kenya (47 per cent) and South Africa (37 per cent) feature highly on this list, as does Finland (37 per cent). At the other end of the scale, France, Romania, Hungary (all 15 per cent), South Korea (18 per cent) and the United States (20 per cent) have much lower levels of newspaper readership.

It is hard to spot universal patterns in data of this kind, not least because we find very different sorts of countries grouped together for different metrics. However, it is clear that – even in countries where it is less used – social media is an increasingly important news source, often rivalling more traditional news providers.

We can also get a sense of how this situation has changed in recent years in a more limited number of countries. When it first started as a smaller survey in 2013, the Reuters Institute Digital News Report asked the same questions it asks today in nine countries. We can look to see how news consumption patterns have changed in these countries over this seven-year period. This data is shown in Figure 1.

Here we can clearly see the dramatic change in news consumption habits in recent years. In all the countries surveyed, television news consumption has decreased, in some cases greatly. In the UK, citizens who get their news from television declined by 24 percentage points (79 per cent in 2013 to 55 per cent in 2020). In Denmark, the decline was 23 percentage points. However, the largest contraction was in print media consumption, which fell in all surveyed countries over the period, but most clearly in Italy and the UK (37 percentage point decline). While online news consumption has remained broadly stable or slightly declined in all countries (aside from Japan, where it has actually contracted by 23 percentage points), social media has been the most important growth

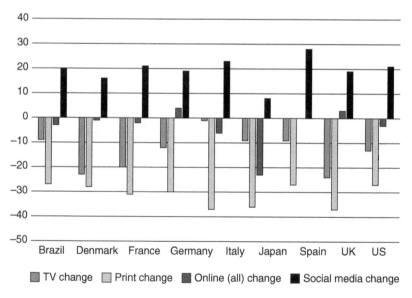

Figure 1 Changes in news consumption in nine countries, 2013–2020

Source: Reuters Institute (2020) Digital News Report

area over the period, increasing everywhere, but notably in Spain (up 28 percentage points), Italy (up 23 percentage points), the United States and France (both up 21 percentage points).

While it might vary from country to country, the general pattern seems to be quite clear: traditional media sources, especially print media, have seen a decline in the number of people they are reaching, while social media has become a major conduit through which citizens get their news.

How does social media change news consumption?

One commonly cited argument is that social media environments under-mine the pluralism of an individual's news consumption, ensuring they only see those ideas and news sources with which they instinctively agree. In contrast, content that challenges their prejudices will never make it onto their newsfeeds. Various versions of this argument have been made, some-times being referred to as Balkanization, filter bubbles or echo chambers (Jamieson & Cappella, 2008; Pariser, 2011; Sunstein, 2001). At the outset, and the despite the prominence of the idea, it should be stated that the empirical evidence for the existence of filter bubbles is very limited.

The logic of the filter bubble argument is twofold. First, on social media, users tend to interact with people they know in the real world, for example their families and friends, or those they encounter in social settings (e.g. places of education or work). People in these groups tend to share similar values and outlooks. As a result, most contact on social media occurs among like-minded individuals. The second factor relates to how social media systems organize content. Every time we interact with the social media environment (by commenting, liking or sharing) the system is learning about our behaviour. Social media sites use this infor-mation to try to predict more accurately what we are going to like and to serve up more content that meets these requirements. The problem here is obvious: behaviour online has the potential to generate feedback loops where users like particular types of content they agree with, and then subsequently see more content that is broadly similar, and very little that challenges their views.

The idea of echo chambers has been closely linked to fake news. The rationale for this is that closed communities, bound together by their ideological prejudices, offer environments that are unlikely to engage critically with untrue stories, particularly if they contain content that besmirches their political opponents. One of the best weapons against inaccurate information circulating – pluralistic critique from across the political spectrum – has been removed.

The idea of filter bubbles makes intuitive sense. However, the evidence for their existence is rather harder to come by. Studies by Facebook data scientists suggest that, in political outlook at least, users have a more diverse set of friends than is usually imagined. Out of every five friends that an individual might have, four of them share the same political outlook, but one will have a different set of views. As a result, users will encounter ideologically diverse content (Bakshy, Messing, & Adamic, 2015). Other studies also suggest that the echo chamber argument can be overstated. Bruns (2019), for example, argues that social media and search engine news users have a more diverse news diet than those who do not use these services.

While we should not get carried away with the concept of filter bubbles, it is worth noting that social media does create quite a different type of news environment from traditional media. While some users of the major platforms actively follow news media corporate accounts (Facebook users 30 per cent; Twitter users 31 per cent) or journalists (10 per cent and 24 per cent respectively), by far the most common reason that users claim to discover news content is because it is trending (54 per cent and 57 per cent) or because it is shared (52 per cent and 41 per cent) or commented on (54 per cent and 41 per cent) by friends in their network (Ofcom, 2020).

We have therefore moved from a situation where news was provided by authoritative media institutions to one where it is increasingly provided by networks of family, friends and acquaintances. Furthermore, the study cited above written by Bakshy et al. (2015) suggests that while users of Facebook do encounter news stories that might not match their personal opinion, they are also 70 per cent less likely to click on those stories than those which conform to their ideological outlook.

Who do we trust to provide our news?

A slightly different but related question is whether people trust the news generally and also news that comes from particular media. The Reuters Institute also gathers data on these questions. The findings are shown in Figure 2. The countries which display the greatest trust in media are eclectic – Finland (56 per cent trust in media, the highest of all countries

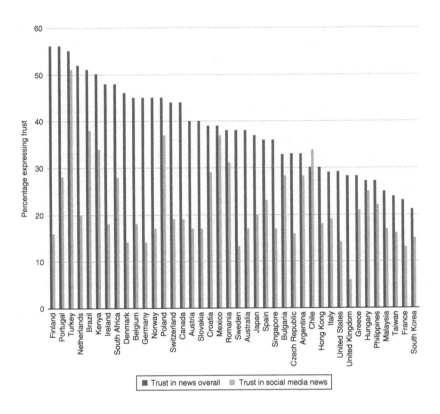

Figure 2 Trust in news and news from social media, 2020

Source: Reuters Institute (2020) Digital News Report

surveyed) and the Netherlands (52 per cent) would generally be regarded as very successful democracies. In contrast, Turkey (52 per cent) and Brazil (51 per cent) have seen significant democratic declines in recent years, but still rank highly according to this metric.

At the other end of the rankings, established democracies like France (23 per cent), the UK (28 per cent) and the United States (29 per cent) show very low levels of trust in media. South-East Asian countries – notably South Korea (21 per cent trust in media, the lowest of the countries surveyed), Taiwan (24 per cent), Malaysia (25 per cent) and the Philippines (27 per cent) – also feature low down on this list.

A pattern starts to become a bit clearer if we examine the second column on the graph, which shows trust in social media as a source of news. We can compare this with trust in news media generally. What we find here is that in a number of countries where the government has authoritarian tendencies, citizens are relatively more likely to trust social media as a source of news. Hungary (only a 2 percentage point difference between trust in media generally and trust in social media news), Turkey (a 4 percentage point difference) and Poland (8 percentage point difference) all feature high up on the list. In contrast, the lower end of this list is made up of countries that are generally regarded as more stable democracies: Finland (40 percentage point difference), Denmark, the Netherlands (both 32 percentage point difference), Germany (31 percentage point difference), Ireland (30 percentage point difference) and Norway (28 percentage point difference).

There are two possible explanations for this, both of which might be occurring simultaneously. The first is that citizens seeking to question and challenge governments with authoritarian tendencies are turning to social media as an alternative source of information because it is harder for officials to censor and control. The second explanation is that social media provides an avenue for government supporters to reject and even attack the traditional media. By looking online, they can find news that is more ideologically conducive to their belief systems.

Data of this kind provides a useful snapshot and comparative insights into media trust. However, three further observations need to be made. First, cited in isolation, some of the figures on levels of trust in media over time appear completely damning. In the United States, for example, Gallup polling recorded a decline from a 68 per cent trust level in 1968 to 32 per cent in 2016. However, it is important to note these numbers did recover somewhat by 2018, increasing to 45 per cent. While the United States has clearly seen an overall trend of declining trust in media, it is important to recognize that this trend is unstable (Jones, 2018). Second, that trend is evident in many countries. However, the extent and speed of that trend does vary in different contexts. Asian countries, for example, seem to be experiencing it at a slower rate than the Anglosphere (Hanitzsch, Van Dalen, & Steindl, 2018).

Third, and perhaps most importantly, measuring trust at this macro level runs the risk of missing something else important that is happening, which is a decline in trust among specific segments of the population for certain parts of the media. There is evidence that strength of partisan feeling is related with a lack of trust in the media, for example (Lee, 2010). If the decline in trust is focused disproportionately on traditional news providers, news consumers may start to look elsewhere for alternative sources of news.

How is our relationship with politics changing?

It would be tempting to conclude our account there. Changing technology – particularly the move from broadcast to digital, from mass to fragmented media, and the decline of gatekeepers – provides a significant part of the explanation for contemporary concerns about fake news. However, while technology-based explanations of this kind are seductive in their simplicity, it is altogether too crude an explanation when deployed in isolation. Political institutions and how citizens relate to them have changed dramatically too.

The great mid-twentieth-century political scientist E. E. Schattschneider wrote that 'The political parties created democracy and modern democracy is unthinkable save in terms of the parties' (1960, p. 1). Certainly, parties have proved themselves the most effective vehicle for constructing democratic engagement at the scale of the modern nation state. Therefore, it makes sense at least partially to equate the health of democracy with the health of parties and party systems.

However, recent years have been spectacularly turbulent for parties and party systems which once appeared to be fixed points of politics in various countries. Old parties that were once dominant have experienced relative decline (the SPD in Germany or Congress in India, for example) or complete collapse (PASOK in Greece). New parties have emerged and grown rapidly in support, either directly influencing policy (UKIP in the UK) or entering government (the Five Star Movement in Italy). Other older parties have suffered hostile takeovers from individuals and factions that were traditionally on the periphery of their movement (Donald Trump's successful campaign for the Republican presidential nomination or Jeremy Corbyn's five-year leadership of the UK Labour Party). Some new parties have successfully emerged after being built entirely around charismatic individuals (En Marche in France). Other long-established parties have formed alliances with their traditional rivals in an effort to maintain their grip on power (grand alliances have been formed between the German

Christian Democrats and Social Democrats, while Fianna Fáil and Fine Gail are currently in a coalition government in Ireland). Across a number of countries, ideologies once on the margins – the radical far-right and Green parties to name two examples – are now achieving unprecedented electoral success.

Why have these changes occurred? A number of explanations have been offered. Some of the countries that have experienced the most radical changes in their party system, such as Greece, were particularly hard hit by the financial crisis which started in 2007, and incumbent political parties were punished by the electorate. However, a broader explanation is offered by the political scientist Peter Mair, who argued that political parties, which had once been constructed on the basis of their relationship to the structural organization of society (i.e. they would represent a particular class or religion), have become hollowed out, technocratic organizations. They no longer had a popular dimension (Mair, 2013). This matters because parties provided an important conduit between the rulers and ruled. Their decline as popular organizations has severed that connection.

This thesis was supported by research from the turn of the century, notably Dalton and Wattenberg's highly influential book *Parties Without Partisans* (2002). However, this prediction may have been premature. While parties appeared to be in decline, many countries saw increased levels of partisanship (defined as the extent to which political issues are viewed through the prism of partisan identification). This was most evident in the United States (Brewer, 2005). An example of the power of partisan identification was evident in the aftermath of the 2020 election, when Donald Trump claimed that the election had been rigged: 90 per cent of Democrats felt the election was fair; in contrast, 70 per cent of Republicans felt that the election was unfair (Kim, 2020).

Parties have not gone away, but instead changed form. They have moved from being top-down mass membership institutions to existing within a wider network (Chadwick, 2007). The party sits within a group of pressure groups, interests, activists and supporters. Within this network, information can be disseminated very rapidly, but there are also more voices. Levels of central control and lines of accountability have declined.

In this sort of environment, it is unsurprising that there is increasing concern about the polarization of politics. Polarization can be thought of as how different sides of a political debate relate to each other and the extent that there is any kind of political consensus between them. At its most extreme, polarization can lead to politics involving two implacably opposed camps. Polarization has been much discussed in American politics in the past two decades, as the possibility of bipartisan responses to policy problems has seemed to recede. That said, it seems to be a broader pattern evident in other countries as well (McCoy & Somer, 2019). Polarization can function at both an elite level, between legislators, and at a more popular level, between party members and voters.

Our final political change is the rise of populism. If one word has captured the political imagination in recent years, it is populism. Populism can be defined through a few characteristics. First, it claims to be a form of political leadership that represents and acts on behalf of the people. Second – in order to do this – it needs to define *the people*. This process will inevitably exclude some groups. This out-group might be the existing political class (i.e. Donald Trump's stated desire to 'drain the swamp' in Washington), an immigrant group (again Trump's attacks on Mexican immigration), a set of political ideas or objectives (the Johnson administration in the UK attacking those who wish to remain in the EU), a particular religious group (non-Hindus and particularly Muslims in Modi's India), or criminals (the focus on drug dealers in the Philippines). It is important to note that populism is not restricted to the political right. The Occupy Movement's slogans of *the 99 per cent vs the 1 per cent* and *Main Street vs Wall Street* also defines an in-group and an out-group.

Taken together, these changes point to the decline of an older form of democracy, sometimes referred to as the technocratic liberal order (Waisbord, 2018). This approach to politics was built on (relative levels of) elite consensus and rational approaches to policy-making. However, in an era of unstable party systems, partisan networks, polarization and populism, this approach to politics appears unsustainable.

The changing form of the party system matters to discussions about fake news for two reasons. First, when political parties were socially grounded, they acted as conduits for political education and socialization. In so doing, they placed boundaries on the acceptable terms of political debate. Second, the instability in party systems described above is both a cause and a symptom of a wider process of political instability that has provided a fertile ground for the circulation of fake news. Polarization creates a politics which is based on believing the worst about your political opponents. Populism divides society up into an in-group and out-group. All of these attributes create an unstable, highly vitriolic form of politics.

What is the relationship between the media and democratic politics?

While the previous two sections have detailed some of the challenges facing both media and political institutions, we also need to examine the relationship between the media and democratic politics. The media is so important to contemporary politics that it has been argued to be a political institution in its own right, comparable with other political institutions, such as parliaments and parties (Schudson, 2002).

What role does the media play in democratic life? The American academic Doris Graber drew on speeches from politicians, writings by prominent constitutional scholars and the texts of significant court rulings to identify five distinct roles that the press – defined by Graber in the broad sense of including both print and electronic media – should theoretically be playing to facilitate democratic politics (Graber, 1986). While the arguments she made drew on the context of the United States, the list Graber came up with would be recognizable in any liberal democracy, even if the way it was institutionalized might be different. The five functions were:

1. **The media as a rational marketplace for ideas.** The media provides a forum where different and conflicting ideas can be debated, and those who hold them can engage with each other. Through this process of deliberative debate, the strengths and weaknesses of different positions can be weighed, and the most rational policy responses emerge.

2. **The media as a source of political information to educate the public.** In order to make informed decisions about politics, including who they are going to vote for, the public need access to relevant information. In modern democracies in large states where few citizens are able to have direct contact with political leaders (as distinct from older models of direct democracy, such as is associated with ancient Greece), it is the media that, in theory at least, can share these details with the public.

3. **The media as the voice of public opinion.** Most obviously, in contemporary reporting, the media gives voice to public opinion through

the publication of opinion polls. But it might equally be reflected, in different ways, through letters pages, vox pop-type features on news programmes, or panel discussion shows where members of the public can engage directly with politicians. Additionally, Graber noted, plenty of politicians equated what appeared in the popular media with what the public might actually think about specific issues, even if there was no evidence linking the two.

4. **The media as protectors of minority rights.** Democracy literally means the rule of the many. But what happens to the minority who disagree? One role of the media is to ensure that their voices are heard, and that they can continue to contribute to debates on key policy issues. In this sense, the media provides an environment where a pluralist range of opinions can be heard, rather than just the voices of the majority.

5. **The media as watchdogs over politicians.** The idea that the media has a role to hold politicians accountable and uncover corruption became particularly established in the popular imagination following the Watergate scandal.

Given this list of objectives, it is easy to see why fake news is considered such a problem. Fake news seems particularly to undermine the media's function in providing information that is required for citizens to make informed, democratic choices.

However, we do need to avoid what is sometimes termed 'golden age-ism'. It was not the case that the media fulfilled all these functions perfectly before the age of Facebook, Trump and fake news. Nor was it the case that citizens were historically perfectly rational decision-makers. In reality, the history of the relationship between media and politics is one of high normative hopes, coupled with empirical disappointment in both the media and the public. Perhaps the best way to think of Graber's list then is as an ideal to aspire to and work towards, rather than something that has ever existed or, for that matter, is ever likely to exist.

Fake news is the latest in the long line of panics about the media and democracy. The previous chapter detailed concern about the yellow press whipping up jingoism. More recent fears go back to the 1970s, when the media was thought to be a destabilizing influence on political institutions, sowing seeds for political conflict by focusing on issues as if they were always subject to binary divisions (Robinson, 1976). In the 1980s, concern grew about television news that seemed to conform more closely to the standards of entertainment than journalistic practice, a genre that became known as infotainment (Postman, 1985). It is not a coincidence that the 1980s also saw a figure from the world of entertainment living in the White House. Politics seemed to be becoming an offshoot of entertainment and the world of celebrity, and this was seen as a cause of concern.[3] More recently, the 1990s and 2000s saw growing disquiet about increasingly polarized and partisan news coverage, particularly related to talk radio and cable television channels such as Fox News.

Voters also rarely live up to the hopes attributed to them in democratic theory. We know, for example, that most citizens have very imperfect political knowledge and generally give politics very limited attention. We also know that when they take political decisions, voters may focus on factors that seem fairly irrelevant in any rational sense. One nice example of this is provided by Christopher Achen and Larry Bartels in their book *Democracy for Realists* (2017). Achen and Bartels examine the 1916 US presidential elections and found there was a negative statistical relationship between the number of votes for incumbent Woodrow Wilson in November 1916 and the coastal New Jersey voting districts which had suffered a series of shark attacks the previous summer, leading to the deaths of four people. This seems the very definition of an irrational voting decision. The Wilson administration could surely not be held responsible for random shark attacks? This did not stop voters in the districts where they occurred from punishing the incumbent.

The shark argument is not uncontroversial, not least because Achen and Bartel's statistical analysis has been criticized (Fowler & Hall, 2018). Furthermore, there are explanations for this voting behaviour, which, while they might not fit into a narrow definition of rationality, do make some sense. The shark attacks became a cultural phenomenon, and were frequently used as metaphors for other things. They were referenced in satirical newspaper cartoons, for example, to show US weakness in face of the German U-boat threat in the Atlantic prior to the country's entry into the First World War. It is conceivable that these sorts of messages were simply felt more keenly in districts that were directly affected by the events that they were referencing.

The logical conclusion of these arguments is that we should be less concerned by fake news. The traditional media hardly has a blemish-free record of providing citizens with political information of the highest quality. Even if citizens were provided with such information, it is questionable if they would be either able or inclined to use it to make good political judgements. However, this argument should not be used as an excuse to avoid acknowledging how the media and political environment is evolving. Traditional gatekeeper-managed sources of news are in decline, and distrusted by significant portions of the population in many countries. To some extent at least, they have been replaced by social media which contains both user-generated content and targeted advertising. Long-established and hierarchical political institutions have decayed, while politics has become increasingly polarized and subject to populist insurgency. It is hard to imagine an environment better for fake news to circulate.

Where does fake news come from?

We now turn our attention to some questions specifically about the phenomenon of fake news. The first question to address is where do the stories that enter circulation actually come from? Broadly, we can identify three motivations for the creation and circulation of fake news: profit, geopolitics, and partisanship/ideology.

Even before polling day in the 2016 US election, journalists had started to write about the town of Veles in Macedonia (Silverman, 2016a). Despite having a population of only about 50,000 people, Veles had become known as the global capital of fake news. The story went like this: teenagers in the town had figured out that they could make money through republishing content about the US election. It did not matter whether the news was real or not. In fact, the more sensationalist, the better. They would copy and paste content, reposting it on numerous crude WordPress-powered websites, and then share the links on social media, particularly on hyperpartisan groups. This in turn would generate audience for their websites, and a proportion of that audience would click on adverts placed on the sites, generating a payment.

In various interviews conducted by journalists with the teenagers from Veles involved in sharing fake news, they were very clear that they had no particular ideological intent, but rather were simply in it to make money. However, it was quickly discovered that it was stories targeted at Donald Trump's supporters that had the greatest tendency to go viral.

The online click-through ecosystem is central to the story about fake news. It is the business model that powers many of the most powerful corporations online. Google AdSense, for example, pays a website every time an advert is clicked on. However, not all clicks are created equal – a click from the United States is worth more than a click from many other parts of the world. Facebook's business model is based wholly on providing a conduit for advertisers to reach consumers who are likely to be interested in their products. The information that users willingly give the site about their interests, hobbies and lives is used to target advertising at them more effectively and make predictions about which users are likely to be interested in which products. In this business environment then, there is a premium on content that can engage people. Whether that content is true or not becomes a secondary concern.

However, the story of amoral teenagers in Macedonia creating fake news is arguably just a bit too comforting. After all, profit seems an altogether less scary motivation than a foreign power attempting to subvert an election or untruths promulgated by an extremist ideology. Besides, as accounts of the activities in Veles have noted, while the content was being shared by Macedonian teenagers, the Facebook pages they were posting links on were created by pre-existing partisan groups online. The divisions that made the creation of fake news such a profitable activity were already well established in American society.

The possibility of exploiting pre-existing divisions is central to the second motivation for the creation of fake news. This is fake news as an aspect of geo-politics. By this, I mean the use of fake news by one state to undermine the institutions, political discourse and social cohesion of another state. Perhaps the most famous example of this type of fake news production is the so-called Internet Research Agency (the IRA) in St Petersburg in Russia. Retrospectively, we know a lot about the IRA's involvement in the 2016 US presidential elections, as its actions were the subject of an investigation led by Robert Mueller, a former Director of the FBI and Special Counsellor to the US Department of Justice (2019). Mueller's report detailed the activities of the IRA, finding a concerted Russian attempt to subvert the electoral process.

In the period prior to the 2016 presidential election, the IRA engaged in a social media campaign to undermine Hillary Clinton, support Donald Trump and escalate pre-existing political divisions. The method deployed was what Howard (2020) refers to as a 'lie machine' – in other words, a vast number of fake social media accounts purporting to be owned by American citizens but actually run by the IRA. These accounts were sometimes controlled by human beings creating content, while other accounts used bots. In this context, a bot is a computerized social media account which automatically produces content, pretending to be human. Bots can be used to mislead the algorithm that social media sites use to organize content, by making topics trend, for example.

Additionally, paid advertising on social media platforms was also employed to target messages at particular groups. In total, the IRA spent $100,000 placing 3,500 different advertisements on Facebook during the course of the election campaign. These adverts were designed to target particular groups among the US electorate, notably conservative Trump supporters and African Americans. It is this combination of organically produced content, bot activity and targeted paid advertising that was central to the IRA's fake news campaign.

The final source of fake news is those who are motivated by ideological or partisan reasons. Despite the attention given to teenagers in Eastern Europe and Russian online operatives, a huge amount of fake news comes from or is disseminated by those at the very top of long-established political institutions in stable democracies. Donald Trump is, of course, the prime exponent of this approach, particularly through his Twitter account. An article published in the *Washington Post* in July 2020 suggested that Trump had told no fewer than 20,000 lies during the course of his presidency (Kessler, Rizzo, & Kelly, 2020). Beyond formal party leaders is a much wider network of content creators and sharers. In Trump's case, this includes his immediate family, but also extends to supportive websites, social media groups, think tanks and independent commentators who share untrue, misleading or heavily spun information. Additionally, a significant role is played by traditional media organizations, which promulgate or at the very least give undue credence to fake news stories (Benkler et al., 2018).[4]

The fake news environment is networked. This leads to a number of important observations about how fake news circulates. First, information can cross boundaries between the various sources of fake news. Macedonian teenagers were copying and pasting content from partisan websites in the United States, while the Mueller report found that members of Trump's family had actually liked content produced by the IRA on Twitter. Many of these stories then crossed over into mainstream news providers.

There is therefore not one source of fake news, nor are the many sources isolated from each other.

Second, both the example of the Russian IRA and the partisan news ecosystem point to an institutional facet that is important to the production and circulation of fake news. Those who are engaged in it are frequently one step removed from the institutions whose interests they serve. The IRA is not formally part of the Russian government, intelligence services or military. Rather, it is a private institution. However, it just happens to be owned by the oligarch Yevgeny Prigozhin (otherwise known as Putin's chef, as he owns catering businesses that have catered state banquets). Similarly, many of the purveyors of partisan or ideological fake news are not actually embedded within the formal institutions of political parties. This model is a reflection of the increasingly networked nature of party and political activity, and has a significant advantage of allowing a greater level of deniability to political elites.

How much fake news is there, who sees it and do they believe it?

What proportion of our news diet is made up of fake news? This is a difficult question to address, and can be approached through a number of methods, none of them perfect. In a high-profile article published on Buzzfeed in the run-up to the 2016 US election, reporter Craig Silverman (2016b) observed that fake news stories outperformed accurate news coming from traditional news providers, measured in terms of the number of interactions they were generating on Facebook. Between August and the election day in November, the top 20 fake news stories generated 8.7 million engagements, compared with the top 20 accurate news stories, which only managed 7.3 million engagements.

An alternative measure is used by Allcott and Gentzkow (2017). Drawing on a variety of sources, they created a database of 156 fake news articles that appeared during the period of the 2016 US election. Allcott and Gentzkow deployed three methods to estimate the circulation of these stories:

1. From various sources, they estimate that the likely upper bound of shares to page visits on Facebook is 20 to 1 (i.e. every time an article is shared, this means that 20 people will view it). The articles in the

database were shared about 38 million times, giving a figure of 760 million page visits. This would be the equivalent to each American adult being exposed to three fake news stories over the course of the election campaign.

2. By drawing on browser data, they estimate that 65 fake news sites received 159 million impressions. This would equate to 0.64 impressions per adult. It is worth noting – and comparing with Silverman's findings – that the same method suggests more reputable news organizations received more than 3 billion page impressions, roughly equivalent to 14.4 page impressions per adult.

3. Finally, using survey recall data, they calculated that the average adult saw 1.14 fake news articles during the course of the election campaign.

Allcott and Gentzkow are also able to use their survey to understand who believes fake news stories. They find that participants who are older, have higher levels of education and consume more news content generally are *more likely* to be able to identify fake news as untrue. Additionally, they find that those who hold a conservative ideology are less likely to be able to accurately identify fake news stories as untrue. However, the same group of people is also more likely to correctly answer that a true news story is accurate when asked in a survey. This suggests that they are overall more credulous, rather than necessarily just more susceptible to fake news.

Guess, Nagler, and Tucker (2019) undertook a study to find out who was more likely to share fake news content on Facebook. Their findings do not necessarily contradict Allcott and Gentzkow's, but suggest some alternative complexities to sharing patterns, as they find that older and conservative-leaning users are *more likely* to share fake content.[5] They also include the important caveat, though, that the sharing of fake news activity on Facebook is a minority pursuit, taking place among relatively small segments of the site's user base.

This work is important, but only scratches the surface of the problem, for a couple of reasons. First, as we have already seen, fragmented media means that citizens can be consuming very different content. Additionally, the attributes of social media make it likely that particular groups will be sharing distinctive content. Users can also receive advertising and information which are heavily tailored to their interests, predispositions and prejudices. This means that fake news and inaccurate information might appear to have a relatively limited presence on the platform overall but may be much more prominent in the media diets of certain sub-groups.

Furthermore, by focusing on individual items of fake news and the propensity of individual users to read or share them, this type of research misses the role played by broader ideas and narratives in the circulation of fake news. This becomes particularly problematic when fake news blends into real news stories. Apart from the infamous Pope endorsing Trump story (the most shared item of fake news in the election), Silverman lists the five top circulating fake news stories from the 2016 election (Silverman, 2016b). The four other stories in the list all relate to Hillary Clinton. Two of them reference the Clinton email server scandal. The problem here is that these particular items of fake news were constructed with reference to a real event and a corresponding FBI investigation. The email scandal was widely covered in the mainstream media (indeed, it could be argued, to an excessive degree). The challenge therefore is that fake news stories do not just exist in isolation but are interconnected with a variety of true and untrue content, ranging across different media sources. Even when traditional media does not actively share fake news, it can provide conditions which make it easier for fake news to circulate.

What are the effects of fake news?

This is perhaps the question that intuitively seems most important when considering fake news. Can exposure to it actually make a difference to citizens' political views and behaviour? This question is particularly pressing when recent elections and referendums in various parts of the world have generated very close results which could have easily gone the other way, but for a handful of votes. In these circumstances, fake news would only need to have a small impact to be decisive.

At the outset, though, it is worth noting something that political scientists have been aware of since the 1940s: despite all the attention they get in the media, and vast energy and (in some countries) financial resources they take up, election campaigns do not seem to matter very much to election outcomes (for an early example of this research see Lazarsfeld, Berelson, & Gaudet, 1948). This argument is known as the *minimal effects thesis*, and it is well documented in several decades of academic research.

The original claim was developed with the use of representative sample surveys, a new methodological innovation in the 1940s.

Voters were asked at the beginning of the campaign who they intended to vote for. They were then surveyed again at the end of the campaign and asked who they had actually voted for. What quickly became apparent was that very few voters actually changed their minds in the course of the campaign, despite the best efforts of politicians to persuade them to. Even now, decades later, the general academic consensus is, at least when measured in terms of getting voters to change their minds, election campaigns are not very successful.[6]

The minimal effects thesis is an important corrective to some of the more overblown claims made about fake news. Too often the discourse surrounding fake news has been very simplistic in its analysis of voters, suggesting that they have a rather sheep-like tendency when responding to political messages. We actually know it is very hard to get voters to change their mind about who they are going to support.

That said, the minimal effects thesis should not be used as an excuse for ignoring the risks posed by fake news. Since the 1940s, revisionist researchers have developed and broadened their definition of campaign effects and looked for alternative impacts that campaigns might be having. This has led to a much larger range of effects being defined that could be occurring due to a campaign. These include:

- **De/mobilization effects.** While it is hard to get voters to change their mind through electoral communication, it seems more likely that campaigns can get citizens who are inclined to support them to engage in particular political actions. The most obvious of these is to get citizens to turn out and actually vote for the candidate they are inclined to support. The reverse of this is a demobilization effect. In other words, campaigns might target voters who are inclined to support their opponents with messages that are aimed at triggering disillusionment and decrease the chances of their turning out to vote.

- **Re-enforcement effects.** Voters may hold beliefs going into an election campaign. However, exposure to campaign messages may lead to them holding these views more strongly.

- **Agenda-setting effects.** Election campaigns can be understood as contests to define the most important issues a country faces. Is the major challenge national security or the provision of healthcare, for example?

• **Framing effects.** While agenda setting is a contest over which issues dominate an election campaign, framing relates to how particular issues are understood. How is a particular policy challenge viewed, and what other issues is it thought to be linked to?

Certainly, scholars researching fake news have been mindful of these alternative types of effects. In their report on the activities of Russia's IRA, Howard, Ganesh, Liotsiou, Kelly, and François argue that the misinformation being circulated had two purposes: 'the IRA sought to energize conservatives around Trump's campaign and encourage the cynicism of other voters in an attempt to neutralize their vote' (2019, p. 32). Here then was an attempt to generate de/mobilization and re-enforcement effects. Furthermore, because the messages were targeted at groups on either side of the partisan divide, the likely overall effect could be an increase in polarization.

This is the limitation of studies that attempt to understand the impact (or non-impact) of fake news at the level of individual voters. The potential of fake news to cause the greatest damage is not at the level of the individual, but instead at the level of political debate and institutions. When wielded as an ideological or geo-political weapon, fake news is designed to amplify pre-existing divisions within a society. In so doing, it undermines public confidence in political institutions, and decreases the possibility of consensus building, making it harder to have robust but civil disagreement.

This is neatly illustrated by the targeting of African Americans during the 2016 election campaign. There is nothing fake about the structural disadvantages faced by this community. Notably, this is found in lower levels of formal educational attainment, lower incomes (even when compared with peers with the same level of education), inferior healthcare access and outcomes, and higher incarceration levels (Edmond, 2020). The Black Lives Matter movement has also drawn attention to the greater risk African Americans face of being the victims of police violence.

In these circumstances then, it is not surprising that the IRA set up a Twitter account and a Facebook page called Blacktivist. In total, the Facebook page received 11.2 million engagements (likes, shares or comments). The aim of the campaign was to amplify pre-existing racial tensions and demobilize African American voters. The account was used to circulate untrue stories, such as claims that police officers had physically assaulted a pregnant African American woman. Most audaciously, the group actually organized real-world protests on American streets, encouraging those who followed the page to turn up at a specific time and place. Whether targeted fake news of this kind actually had any electoral effect remains unclear, but it is worth noting that since the 1960s, African Americans have been a vital part of the Democratic Party's electoral coalition. As a result, any demobilization among this group would inevitably have harmed Hillary Clinton's candidacy.

The same playbook was deployed in the 2020 US election. As early as the summer of 2020, Twitter was shutting down fake accounts which purported to belong to an African American voter who had always supported the Democrats but – having seen the 'Marxist' extremism of Black Lives Matter – had decided to change the habit of a lifetime, and back Donald Trump and the Republicans (Collins, 2020). Needless to say, this account was entirely fake and the story it was spreading had no grounding in reality.

What don't we know about fake news?

This chapter has been focused on what we know about fake news. But we finish with a different question, of equal importance: what don't we know about fake news? It is often hard for researchers to obtain data from the types of settings where fake news circulates, particularly online environments. The challenge of researching these environments becomes clear if we compare them with older forms of media.

The contents of newspapers and broadcast television were the same for everyone who consumed them and was publicly available, so they could be archived easily. Contrast this with social media sites, where everyone's timeline contains curated content, driven by the algorithm that responds to a user's unique actions and information on the site. Individual users' timelines are often not publicly accessible. The content is ephemeral (i.e. it does not have a permanent existence). Think of your own social media pages. When you sign into them or refresh them, they look different each time. They cannot be reconstructed retrospectively for the purposes of research (or at least, it is very hard to do so).

Social media companies are reluctant to make this private content public, at least in a useful form. There are two reasons for this. The first is often stated publicly by social media companies – that is, there are questions that surround the privacy of users and their data (for a further discussion of these issues, see Bernal, 2020). By revealing content, the companies would also be revealing private data. This is problematic, they argue, as it makes it harder for them to refuse requests from repressive regimes for data. We might be slightly sceptical about this explanation. The very essence of most social media companies' business models is to employ user data to conduct targeted advertising. This hardly demonstrates a great concern for privacy.

Therefore, the alternative explanation might be more convincing. If too much data were given away, it would reveal the intellectual property of the companies and possibly help their rivals. Social media companies use data to sell advertising that is targeted at individuals who are likely to be responsive to it. Essentially, their ability to do this *is their product*. Revealing data could potentially allow these processes to be reverse engineered, endangering their business.[7]

There are really two ways researchers can access and understand content on social media. The first is to work with social media companies. However, this presents challenges. Following the scandals of 2016, Facebook attempted to create an independent foundation, called Social Science One, which would allow researchers access to Facebook content. However, the organization soon became mired in controversy, with many of the academics involved publicly complaining that Facebook was moving far too slowly in releasing data (de Vreese et al., 2019).

An alternative approach is to open up data through something called an API (an application programming interface). This means that social scientists are able to download data direct from a web service without having to interact with or seek permission from the provider (or, if they do need permission, the process is very perfunctory). The quantity of data that can be obtained from an API tends to be related to the social norms of the network. Twitter user pages are largely public, so historically Twitter has had a fairly open API, allowing the download of significant amounts of real-time data. In contrast, Facebook is a largely private network, with the majority of users setting up their pages so as they can only be seen by those they have friended. Until August 2018, Facebook did have an API that allowed researchers to download data from publicly available Facebook pages. However, this was only a small percentage of the data that was actually available on Facebook.

However, since August 2018, researchers have been even less well served by Facebook, with even the limited API options previously available being scaled back. The paradox here is that the events of 2016, and particularly the illegal use of data by the political consultancy Cambridge Analytica, have actually caused Facebook to make it harder for researchers to access the data they need to understand the role that Facebook is playing in politics.

Trying to identify solutions to the problem of fake news requires the knowledge that can only be generated by access to this sort of rich data from social media platforms. Without it, we can only ever have a partial knowledge of what is actually happening online and how fake news is circulating.

Notes

1. The press did on occasion reference FDR's physical disability, which was the result of polio. However, the narrative when it was mentioned was about his triumph over the disease (Pressman, 2013).
2. The debates about the providence of this story have raged for a number of decades, with academics unable to trace any contemporary evidence for the finding (Vancil & Pendell, 1987). However, more recent experimental studies, where participants either watched or listened to the 1960 debates and were then asked for their opinions on the candidates, have found different responses between the audiences (Druckman, 2003).
3. This comparison is not entirely fair on Ronald Reagan, who had extensive political experience before becoming President. He had served as President of the Screen Actors Guild and was a two-term Governor of California. Prior to winning the presidency, Trump had held no political position of any kind.
4. In their study of the United States, Benkler et al. argue that this is a particular problem on the political right, with more mainstream broadcasters, such as Fox News, sharing rather than challenging fake stories that emerge in far-right online spaces. They further argue that the same patterns do not occur on the American left. It is worth noting, though, that in the aftermath of the 2020 presidential election, all networks (including Fox News) cut away from a live Trump press conference due to his misleading claims about the election being 'stolen' (Grynbaum & Hsu, 2020).

5. The finding about conservatives is not uncontroversial. Other studies have found that Americans who define their politics as extremely liberal are also likely to share fake news (Hopp, Ferrucci, & Vargo, 2020).

6. It is worth noting that the academic research is less clear on referendum campaigns. In normal election campaigns, at least some voters will have a history of partisan identification which makes their voting intentions more stable. In referendums, partisan cues may be absent or confused, which means the campaign is potentially more important (de Vreese, 2007). This may be particularly true when elites do not divide neatly along party lines in a referendum campaign, as occurred in the 2016 UK EU membership vote.

7. Although in a slightly different space, Amazon recently provided an example of how jealously companies guard information about users. In early summer 2020 the company stopped putting details of the items that customers had ordered in emails confirming orders and delivery. The likely reason for this seems to be the cumulative information that companies that provided email (notably Google) could harvest from these emails and then use to compete with Amazon (Smith, 2020).

what should we do?

There are a number of solutions that have been proposed to the problem of fake news. For the purposes of this chapter, I am going to divide these solutions into two distinct types. First, I will examine what can be termed policy-based solutions. By this, I mean particular actions or reforms that can be introduced by corporations, government or civil society groups. These might have a very immediate effect (as is the case with identifying and removing fake news as it appears online) or operate over a much longer term (developing school curricula that improve citizens' digital literacy and ability to recognize fake news stories). In this section, we consider four possible policy-based solutions to fake news: social media sites changing the way they organize and publish content; new forms of government regulation (including a requirement that fake news is removed); fact-checking-style journalism; and improved media literacy education for citizens.

Second, I examine what can be termed discursive solutions. This approach draws on ideas from discursive institutionalism in political science. This is a form of institutional analysis which argues that political institutions are defined not just by the formal rules that govern them, but also by how they are thought about and understood (Schmidt, 2010). In the context of the debate about fake news, taking a discursive approach would involve challenging and adjusting the way we think about news and information in political life. This chapter considers three options that could help: stop talking about fake news altogether; rejecting the arguments made by postmodernist scholars; and rethinking our relationship with demo-cratic institutions. Of all the solutions, I argue, it is the last – rethinking our relationship with democratic institutions – which is most promising.

Social media sites changing their relationship with content

The first solution which we can explore relates to how social media sites manage, organize and police the content that appears on their platforms. However, it should be noted that social media sites have been remarkably reticent about getting involved in this sort of activity. There are a number of reasons for this.

The first issue relates to how social media companies define them-selves. Historically, they have (largely successfully) argued that they are not publishers, but platforms which provide a space for their users to cre-ate and share content. A good way of thinking about this is the difference between a telephone company (a platform) and a newspaper (a publisher). If I use a telephone to spread slanders about someone, the phone com-pany has no legal liability for what I have said. If, on the other hand, I write something libellous in a newspaper, the newspaper has a legal responsibil-ity for the content. Arguably, the events of 2016 have made this position increasingly unsustainable for social media companies. Speaking before a Congressional Committee exploring the role of social media in US politics, Mark Zuckerberg admitted that:

> [I]t's clear now that we didn't do enough to prevent these tools from being used for harm as well. That goes for fake news, foreign interfer-ence in elections and hate speech, as well as developers and data pri-vacy. We didn't take a broad enough view of our responsibility, and that was a big mistake. It was my mistake. (Quoted in Rushe, 2018)

Zuckerberg's history is slightly disingenuous: social media sites have fre-quently removed and moderated content. Famously, Facebook has long had an anti-(female) nipple rule, which has led to controversies surround-ing nude works of art and images of women breastfeeding being removed from the site. However, the challenge for Facebook is neatly summed up in another issue created by the nipple rule: the removal of images of topless political protestors. When Facebook has removed these images under its community standards policy, it has been accused of political censorship (Paul, 2019).[1]

This leads us to a more convincing argument against social media companies being involved in identifying and removing fake news. This sort of activity would require them to engage in highly controversial political and editorial judgements that they are simply not equipped for. Indeed, given the sheer quantity of content appearing on social media platforms, it seems almost foolhardy to entrust individual corporations with this amount of power.

Certainly, for long periods of their history, Facebook and Twitter have been very wary of making decisions which might make it look as if they were getting involved in politics and elections (BBC News, 2019). However, there are signs that this policy is gradually shifting. In May 2020, Twitter flagged a tweet from Donald Trump related to rioting in Minneapolis. Trump used the site to threaten to send in the National Guard and, in a second tweet, added that 'when the looting starts, the shooting starts'. Whether wittingly or not, the President was quoting a Florida Police Chief who had used the same phrase when advocating racialized policing in 1967. Twitter did not remove the tweet. However, it did put a content warning on it, informing users that the content breached the site's code of conduct (BBC News, 2020). Later, during the coronavirus pandemic, both Facebook and Twitter took a much more robust line with Trump, removing content where the President claimed that children were largely immune to the disease (Bond, 2020). Decisions like this create a challenge for social media companies, though, as Trump and his supporters very quickly accused them of displaying bias against the President in particular and right-wing ideas in general. Congressional Republicans suggested increased regulation targeted at the companies.

The argument that social media companies should not become involved in shaping political and electoral content is misconceived. It implies they are not doing this already. The reality is rather different. The design decisions taken by companies like Facebook play a huge role in deciding what content appears on users' timelines. Social media companies are seeking to maximize engagement with content on their sites, as this in turn maximizes their profits. Furthermore, proactive decisions can be – and already are being – taken to reorder the content users are seeing and downgrade disinformation (Hutchinson, 2018).

The future of fake news management on social media sites is likely to be a combination of these two approaches: high-profile takedowns, leading to accusations of bias, coupled with more subtle changes, tweaking the way in which content is presented to users.

Government responses

If we collectively recognize that fake news poses a serious threat to politics and societal stability, and social media platforms seem unlikely to act to tackle the problem, then maybe it is the role of governments to intervene? As we shall see, some countries have actually attempted this, with mixed success. The extent to which such an approach is even politically possible depends greatly on the history and political culture of a particular country. How such a policy is enacted and who has responsibility for this process also raise other complex questions.

In 2017, Germany passed the Network Enforcement Act (NetzDG). This gave the country some of the strongest laws in the world for the policing of fake news and illegal content. The headline-grabbing aspect of the new law was that social media networks would have 24 hours to remove what was termed 'obviously illegal' content or face fines of up to €50 million (sites are granted seven days to remove content that is merely 'illegal').

This is unsurprising for historical reasons. Since 1949, the Federal Republic of Germany has had a strongly shared national consensus that it was both desirable and necessary to control some forms of information and symbols, notably those related to the Nazi past (although the same legislation also covers communist symbols and more recently flags associated with ISIS). The German criminal code also specifically outlaws Holocaust denial, leading to a number of high-profile prosecutions. These laws are specifically in place to safeguard the constitutional order of the Federal Republic and shape public understanding of German history (Art, 2005).

However, in practice, the German model of policing social media content has proved very controversial. It has been attacked by civil society groups, and been accused of breaching the country's constitution (the Basic Law) as a disproportionate imposition on freedom of speech. Since the punishments are so punitive, it can lead to far too much content being taken down by risk-averse social networks. As a result, the law is now being reviewed (Thomasson, 2018). Even if the German approach did work, it would not be appropriate everywhere. In other countries, notably the United States, the constitution makes it much harder to limit free speech rights. As a result, legislation of this kind would likely be ruled as unconstitutional by the Supreme Court.

There are other consequences of this sort of government regulation in liberal democracies. It can provide cover for authoritarian regimes and repressive populists around the world in their own efforts to increase the levels of censorship in their societies. Belarus, for example, passed legislation in June 2018 allowing the government to prosecute people who spread so-called false information online and block the website which hosted it. Certainly, laws of the kind operating in Germany, however well intentioned, make it much harder for Western countries to critique the censorship practices of other less democratic regimes.

Government responses do not need to be as draconian as the German model. Alternative forms of regulation do exist. These can also be autonomous of government. One approach would be to create an independent regulator, charged with examining the efforts of social media companies to manage fake news and undertaking independent research to better understand the challenge it poses (Truth Trust and Technology Commission, 2018). An alternative approach would be to use legislation to instigate public service requirements for social media platforms. While the most obvious example of public service media in the UK is the BBC, we would not need to go as far as turning Facebook into a statutory corporation.[2] Private media can also have public service obligations – for example, to carry news content, religious or children's programmes, and provide equal coverage during the course of an election campaign. Similar requirements could be imposed on social media companies through legislation.

Fact checking

One response to fake news which has been widely attempted is fact checking. A recent academic article on fact checking defined it as 'the practice of systematically publishing assessments of the validity of claims made by public officials and institutions with an explicit attempt to identify whether a claim is factual' (Walter, Cohen, Holbert, & Morag, 2019, p. 2). In various parts of the world, both traditional news outlets and new media startups have taken up fact checking with gusto. The Reporters' Lab at Duke University in the United States maintains a census of active fact-checking organizations around the world. In late 2019, it identified no fewer than 210 fact checkers working across 68 countries. To put this into some historical perspective, when the census was first carried out in 2014, 59 fact-checking organizations were found (Stencil & Luther, 2019). It is not a coincidence that increasing levels of fact checking have directly paralleled concern about fake news. Certainly, in many quarters, fact checking has been viewed as an important response to inaccurate information that is in circulation. But does it actually work? There are a number of reasons to be doubtful.

Most of the evidence for the effectiveness of fact checking comes from experimental studies, where academics show participants news media content in a laboratory and carry out surveys after this exposure (e.g. Porter, Wood, & Kirby, 2018). However, this method necessarily removes much of the political and communicative complexity that exists outside the lab. In a real-world setting, fact checking starts to look rather less effective. Three problems are apparent.

First, there is the practical challenge of reach and audience. Who actually consumes the fake news and who actually sees the fact check that corrects the inaccuracies? If a false claim is made by a politician appearing on a major news programme, for example, a broadcaster might then use its website to publish a fact check of what was said. However, this is likely to reach a far smaller proportion of citizens than did the original inaccurate claim.

Second, the genre of fact-checking websites is ripe for imitation and politicization. During the first TV leaders' election debate in the UK in 2019, the Conservative Party renamed its Twitter account as factcheckUK. During the course of the broadcast, the account was used to attack Jeremy Corbyn, the leader of the opposition Labour Party. While the Conservatives claimed that the account was still labelled, they had changed the whole branding of the site and dropped their distinctive blue colouring or any other party identifiers. This action was widely criticized, leading to Twitter issuing a warning to the party saying that any repeat would lead to their being barred from the site (Perrigo, 2019). Whether the Conservative stunt was effective or not, it highlights the ease with which fake fact-checking sites could be used to seed even more confusion within public debate.

Third, it is possible that at times fact checking and the publicity that surrounds it can make the original inaccurate claims more effective. One example of this occurring was the infamous claim made by Vote Leave in the 2016 UK EU membership referendum campaign that leaving the EU would give the UK an extra £350 million per week, which could be spent on the National Health Service. This claim was untrue in various ways. The UK had a rebate from the EU, which meant that the weekly cost of membership was nearer £250 million. Additionally, much of this money was then returned to the UK under various EU schemes (e.g. through regional support, higher education and agriculture). Given that the Vote Leave campaign had also suggested that the UK should replace these schemes in the event of leaving the EU, much of the money was simply not there to be spent on the NHS (or, if it was, it would come at the expense of other promises the campaign had made). Finally, the vast majority of economic forecasting suggested that the UK outside the EU would be less productive, leading to a decline in tax revenue. As a result, Brexit would mean that there would likely be less money for public services, not more.

There followed a rhetorical battle between the Vote Leave campaign and public organizations (including the UK Statistics Authority, who reprimanded the campaign) as well as a variety of fact-checking websites. Perhaps surprisingly, though, Vote Leave were thrilled with the publicity this generated (Shipman, 2016, pp. 254–255). The £350 million figure may have been controversial, but even the fact checkers looking to correct it were citing numbers that must have seemed astronomic to the average member of the public. The fact-checking website Full Fact, for example, concluded that the actual figure was 'more like £250 million' because of the rebate (Full Fact, 2017). The row over factual accuracy just ensured that a variety of very large figures were repeated throughout the campaign, while technical questions about government accounting and how to calculate the cost of membership distracted from much larger structural questions about the challenges Brexit posed to the British state.

Improving media literacy

Equipping citizens with the skills to engage critically with media and identify fake news when they encounter it is an alternative approach. This policy is sometimes likened to an inoculation against fake news. Like a vaccination, it involves taking pre-emptive actions to protect individuals from fake news when they encounter it. There are actually a variety of literacies citizens could be educated in. A study by Jones-Jang et al. (2019) identified four different types of literacy. These were:

1. Media literacy relates to understanding how news is produced. This involves recognizing that different news media organizations may have distinctive ideological or business agendas shaping how they report news.

2. Information literacy has developed in response to new information environments online. It particularly focuses on developing the skills that are required to access, evaluate and judge information.

3. News literacy focuses on the relationship between news and the role that citizens play in democratic societies, as well as identifying the tensions between objective reporting and value judgements.

4. Digital literacy particularly emphasizes the way in which online news is constructed, recognizing the greater role played by user-generated content, and the blurring of lines between producers and consumers of news.

Using these various forms of literacy, Jones-Jang et al. conduct a survey experiment to identify the most effective strategies for tackling fake news. They find that only one form of literacy – information literacy – is significantly correlated with the ability to identify fake news. They theorize that it is citizens who are information literate who are most able to keep up with the fast-changing online environment, adapting their news consumption habits as the internet evolves and constantly using their online skills to cross-check the information they are reading.

While this is a positive finding, it raises the more complex question of how the teaching of information literacy can be institutionalized. As educationalists writing on the topic have argued (Mason, Krutka, & Stoddard, 2018), simply adding exercises to the school curriculum where students identify real and fake news stories is not sufficient. Rather, a much broader discussion about our ideas of truth and how it relates to politics is required.

Stop talking about fake news

I now turn my attention to what I have termed discursive solutions to the problem of fake news. The first such solution may seem somewhat surprising. Specifically, it has been argued that we should just stop talking about fake news. This argument has taken a number of forms. Some policy-makers have claimed that fake news is too imprecise a term to be used meaningfully in public debate, so should be dropped (House of Commons Digital, Culture, Media and Sport Committee, 2019). The philosopher Joshua Habgood-Coote (2019) develops this argument further in his article 'Stop Talking About Fake News', making three points. First, that fake news is an unstable term with no fixed meaning. This makes it less useful for public discourse. Second, the term is unnecessary because there are already other terms that can be used interchangeably with fake news. Third – and most importantly – the term fake news has now been coopted by both authoritarian states and populist politicians to attack their political opponents. As a result, even well-intentioned uses of the term will have the effect of bolstering these anti-liberal uses of fake news. As a result, we should stop talking about fake news.

This argument is not just theoretical. A study based on experimental data found that when people are exposed to politicians talking about fake news (even if those politicians are attacking genuine disinformation), it increased their levels of distrust in the media (Van Duyn & Collier, 2019).

So, should we just stop talking about fake news? As was discussed at length in the introduction to this book, it is hard to define fake news accurately. However, if social scientists stopped talking about concepts because they were hard to define or contested, we would very quickly run out of things to examine. The lack of an accepted definition does not mean that discussion is not worthwhile. The process of defining the concept and engaging in debate about it forces us to problematize and develop both our theoretical and empirical understanding. The argument offered in this book is that exploring the ambiguities surrounding the meaning of fake news – and particularly its double meaning as both misleading information and populist rhetorical device – points towards a broader crisis in liberal democratic engagement. Understood in these terms, the discussion has the potential to be fruitful.

Stop being postmodern (or possibly be more postmodern?)

Some commentators have linked the rise of fake news with the environment created by postmodernist thought. What is postmodernism and why does it get this blame?

It is hard to offer a single definition of postmodernism. Rather, it is a set of interconnected but distinct ideas spanning a range of academic disciplines, including (but certainly not limited to) the visual arts, architecture, literature, linguistics, politics, and communication studies. To attempt to draw these diverse ideas together is beyond the scope of this book (for a useful introduction to the various strands of postmodernism see Butler, 2002). However, some general tendencies among postmodernist thinkers are of particular interest to a discussion of fake news.

Postmodernists ask questions about power and authority. To take a classic postmodern argument, what is it that defines great art? It is not, postmodernists would argue, some innate quality in an object such as a painting or a sculpture. Rather, it is defined by institutions of the art world and the choices they make. Prestigious art galleries decide what artefacts are worthy of display, for example. Postmodern artists have challenged the distinction between the artwork and the environment which displays it. In the Museum of Contemporary Art in Los Angeles, artist Chris Burden took this idea to an extreme form, constructing a work of art which involved digging up the gallery's floor and exposing the foundations of the building, making the art and the gallery indistinguishable from each other (Burden, 1986).

This type of argument has important ramifications for broader ideas about truth, power, objective reality and the news. In 1995, French postmodernist Pierre Baudrillard published his provocatively titled book *The Gulf War Did Not Take Place* (Baudrillard, 1995). The argument of this short collection of essays is frequently misunderstood. Baudrillard was not claiming that there was no military conflict in Iraq in 1990-91. Rather, he was arguing that what happened on the battlefield was closer to a massacre than a war. This was particularly due to the massive deployment of overwhelming Allied airpower to obliterate Iraqi forces from a distance. The idea that there was a war (as the term is normally understood, with two sides engaged in a fight on a battlefield) was a narrative constructed post hoc through carefully managed public relations by the Allied powers and media coverage of the conflict.

What really concerned Baudrillard, in common with many postmodernists, was the power of language and narratives to shape perceptions of reality. Indeed, taken to its logical extreme, postmodernist thought suggests that language and narratives are all that matters. This has huge ramifications for historians, as it turns history from a process of uncovering what happened in the past into little more than a form of literature or story-telling (Evans, 2012). Even science is not immune from the postmodernist critique. Scientists after all seek to discover universal laws in the physical world, exactly the sort of thing that postmodernists have doubts about. Here, the postmodernist argument is that the way in which scientific dis-covery progresses is not neutral, nor are the language and metaphors that are used to explain scientific theories. Both are shaped by the underlying power relations of society (Butler, 2002, pp. 36–42).

It is perhaps surprising that this argument is so controversial. The idea that the history of scientific discovery is shaped by the interests of par-ticular sections of society and their ability to wield power is hard to argue against. It is difficult to imagine the moon landings happening outside the context of the Cold War, and their eventual success was as much symbolic as scientific. Proof of the symbolic significance of the landing is provided by the effort NASA put into ensuring it would appear as if the Stars and Stripes flag was actually fluttering on the airless lunar surface (the flag the astronauts took with them was braced with a horizontal metal pole).

That said, postmodernist critiques of science run the risk of exposing the approach to ridicule. First, it can start to look like the subject of the attack is the validity of the actual discoveries themselves, rather than the institutions and processes that govern scientific discovery and communi-cation. Second, taken to its extremes, the postmodernist critique can get rather silly, with important and complex scientific discoveries understood only in political or metaphorical terms. It was this tendency that led to the so-called Science Wars of the 1990s, which reached their climax in the Sokal Affair of 1996, where physicist Alan Sokal submitted a spoof paper to a leading postmodernist journal. While the paper adopted a style of prose common in postmodernist writing, its content was essentially non-sensical. This did not stop the paper being accepted for publication. Sokal claimed that this was proof that the postmodern critique of science was more concerned with ideology than serious enquiry (Ross, 1996).

If postmodernist claims that academic history, and even science is based on stories rather than facts, where does this leave news and jour-nalism? This is precisely the question that opponents of postmodernism have raised in the debate about fake news. The centre–right magazine *StandPoint* explicitly linked the two concepts, claiming that by reject-ing the idea of truth, postmodernism opened up the route to fake news (O'Hear, 2020). Academics have also made similar arguments, suggesting that postmodernist thought has provided the inspiration for the purveyors of fake news, even if this is not what its original creators intended (McIntyre, 2018).

This type of claim runs the risk of repeating the errors of the Science Wars three decades ago – namely, tackling an imagined version of postmodernism defined by the most extreme, provocative or contrarian scholarship produced by the approach. Indeed, some postmodern ideas may actually help us better understand the challenge of fake news.

The most important early work in the postmodernist school is Lyotard's *The Postmodern Condition* (1984). Lyotard argues that the postmodern world is defined by the decline of totalizing grand narratives, such as Christian theology or Marxist ideas about class and history. These grand narratives were important because they bound people to shared understandings of the world. In their absence, the way in which different groups within society arrive at their beliefs about what is true becomes progressively more fractured and contested. As a result, the whole idea of truth becomes increasingly subject to political and economic power.

Lyotard is describing something that looks very like the situation in which fake news now circulates. If he can be criticized for anything, it might be that Lyotard was slightly premature in writing off grand narratives. Islamic fundamentalism or resurgent nationalism, for example, have played an important role in creating an environment where fake news can circulate so rapidly.

Postmodernist scholarship can certainly be censured for focusing on critique at the expense of thinking about ways in which information and the validity of arguments could systematically be studied and weighed against each other. It can also be criticized for adopting a dense and unclear communication style, the consequence of writing largely for an audience of like-minded academics. In turn, this allowed postmodernist work to be mischaracterized by its opponents. But postmodernism should not be taken as an attack on the idea of truth. Rather, it is an account of how truth is constructed and how, in an increasingly complex world, these processes have become destabilized. At the very least then, it offers a good diagnosis of the challenges we currently face. Furthermore, in their focus on narratives, postmodernists point towards a vital ingredient in constructing successful democratic institutions. Citizens need to have a common belief in their worth and fairness of these institutions. It is to this I now turn my attention.

Rethink our relationship with democratic institutions

As we have seen in the previous chapter, contemporary democratic institutions face a number of deep-rooted and fundamental problems. These relate both to the media through which citizens get their information and to the forms that contemporary politics is taking.

In order to build trust, the public need to have confidence in the way elections are administered and the processes of political communication need to be made more transparent. A good starting point is to fix the relatively small things, ensuring that the institutional machinery which runs elections is in good order. Many of the changes required are rather mundane, even if they are actually quite hard to bring about: for example, building more effective electoral regulation, reimagined to reflect a world where a significant amount of political activity and news consumption occurs online.

The challenge is that this sort of change is very slow moving. As an example of this, in the UK there have been campaigns for a number of years calling for imprints (i.e. a statement about who purchased an item) to appear on online election adverts purchased by parties and candidates. This would bring online adverts in line with offline campaigning literature. At the time of writing, the regulation is still being discussed with the government promising that legislation will appear at some point in the future (Johnson, 2020). More broadly, electoral regulators need to be given the resources, expertise and powers required to monitor and police contemporary political campaigns.

Beyond this sort of institutional housekeeping, the idea of tackling fake news can be rather overwhelming. After all, this is a policy problem which appears to require taking on the combined might of Facebook and the Russian state, both institutions that are seemingly beyond the reach of national sovereign authority. But this is the wrong way of thinking about the challenge. The destructive power of fake news comes from the interaction of various actors, not from any one group of protagonists, and the roots of the problem are far closer to home. Invariably, the ability of either teenagers in Macedonia or the IRA in St Petersburg to circulate fake news is built on the divisions in the particular society which is being targeted. An extension of this is that if those divisions could to some extent be healed, then the damage that can be done by fake news decreases dramatically.

Fake news thrives in environments where citizens feel excluded from political and democratic processes. It is not a coincidence that in both the election of Donald Trump and the Brexit referendum, significant numbers of citizens turned up to vote who had not been near a polling booth for a number of election cycles. One estimate suggested that 2.8 million citizens who were normally non-voters turned out in the EU membership referendum. The majority of them voted to leave the EU (Hughes, 2019). We can of course attribute this sudden mobilization to fake news and disingenuous promises made by politicians. But a different way of asking the question is why had no other political campaigns successfully engaged these people for decades?

Conclusion

In tackling the problem of fake news, we cannot wish ourselves back to the past. The age of mass-mediated, highly institutionalized democracy has gone. Instead, the challenge we are now facing is to reimagine what successful public communication could look like in an age of a more fragmented society and media. Tackling this is a vast task, but at this point, it would be worth mentioning some general principles which could be used as the starting point for this endeavour. I would highlight three: working to close divisions which have fostered fake news within societies; constructing a renewed form of pluralism in debate; and embedding empathy within politics.

First, and as I have noted throughout this volume, fake news does not create divisions, but rather catalyses pre-existing political and social conflict. It is these divisions – whether social-economic, religious or racial – that provides the raw fuel for fake news. Tackling these inequalities will greatly undermine the purveyors of fake news.

Second, the rise of fake news forces us to rethink the idea of pluralism. Indeed, fake news can be understood as a crisis of pluralism. In other words, the managed pluralism of the mass media era has decayed into the relativism of contemporary political debate. This has created a situation where individuals and groups have constructed their own systems of truth, resistant to external critique and tests of validity. It is not the case that the old system of managed pluralism was perfect. Plenty of groups of citizens (for example ethnic minorities) were excluded by it. Recognizing that there are different perspectives on the truth is not the same as rejecting the idea of truth altogether. The current question is instead how to construct and manage a new pluralist system that gives due weight to various individuals and groups in society, but also allows their arguments to be subjected to external critique.

Finally, the role of empathy in politics urgently needs to be rethought. The collapse of political debate into relativism is bound up in a lack of empathy, and in particular the in-group and out-group political rhetoric employed by populist politicians. A renewed pluralism will be very hard to achieve without a parallel recognition that politicians and citizens can disagree with each other, but simultaneously hold their beliefs for good and honest reasons. As such, increased empathy needs to be at the heart of any project of democratic renewal.

Notes

1. Under the current policy, all of the examples cited – nude art, breastfeeding and political protest – would now be exempt from removal (Facebook, 2020).
2. The nationalization of Facebook has been suggested in some quarters, on the grounds that provides a public good (Howard, 2012).

5

conclusion

On 4 November 2008, nearly a quarter of a million people gathered in Grant Park, Chicago. They had come to hear President-Elect Barack Obama deliver his victory speech. Obama's electoral triumph was historic for many reasons. In the contest for the Democratic Party nomination, he had defeated Hillary Clinton in the most competitive and closely fought primary process of modern times, while his victory over John McCain in the presidential election ensured that Obama became the first African American to win the White House.

There are a variety of reasons why Obama beat Clinton and McCain. However, most accounts would suggest that at least some of his success was down to his campaign effectively employing new forms of communication technology (Lai Stirland, 2008). Obama's team harnessed the internet to mobilize supporters, to organize direct contact campaigning and to fundraise on an unprecedented scale. Furthermore, Obama's supporters used the same technologies to create self-organized networks to act on behalf of their candidate. The Facebook group 1 Million Strong for Obama (which did not quite manage a million supporters but did get to more than 800,000 members by election day) was not set up by the campaign but founded by a university administrator who was inspired when Obama visited his campus. This seemed to be a new sort of campaign, with at least some control decentralized to activists and supporters.

Obama's election victory is arguably the high point of the period that lasted from approximately 2004 (when Howard Dean's internet-fuelled candidature for the Democratic nomination burned bright then fizzled out) to 2011 (the year of the Arab Spring, a series of revolutionary events in the Middle East that were frequently linked to the organizing potential of social media). During this period, new technologies were widely seen as having the potential both to improve existing democracies and to democratize authoritarian regimes.

Just eight years after Obama's victory speech in Grant Park, though, the world looked a very different place. Donald Trump had just won the presidency. His campaign was associated with fake news, Russian electoral meddling, bots inciting online tensions, and negative advertising designed to demobilize specific segments of the electorate. It very quickly became clear that the new President was going to govern as he campaigned – within hours of taking office, his aides were issuing inaccurate information about the number of people attending his inauguration (Hirschfeld Davis & Rosenberg, 2016).

Trump was not alone. Around the world, a series of political and electoral events bought populist politicians to power, and undermined established political institutions and democratic norms. Britain voted to leave the EU in a referendum campaign mired in accusations of lying and corruption. The Philippines, Turkey and Brazil all elected authoritarian 'strongman' leaders. Right-wing governments in Hungary and Poland sought to assert control over independent media and the judiciary. In India, the anti-Muslim rhetoric of the Bharatiya Janata Party (BJP) triggered sectarian violence of the kind not seen for decades. Where politics of this type was successful, discussion of fake news was rarely far behind.

As a result, the internet had gone from being the great hope for those seeking democratic renewal to an unpredictable wreaking ball, wildly swinging around long-established and seemingly stable political institutions.

The optimism surrounding the Obama campaign was not wrong. The two narratives – hope and crisis – can both simultaneously be true. The complex consequences of the development of the printing press indicate that new technologies can be harnessed for seemingly contradictory purposes. There are reasons, though, to think that democratic crisis of which fake news is an important component has the potential to get worse.

The central argument of this book has been that we need to move away from thinking about fake news as content – neatly captured gobbets of information which can be defined as true or untrue. Rather, we need to think more broadly about how we build democratic institutions and practices that are capable of withstanding an age where information and the authority to share that information are more diffusely distributed.

There are other more troubling reasons why we need to go beyond thinking about fake news simply as content. Fake news does not exist simply as words and images online, but is linked to real-world violence and can play a role in radicalizing individuals to engage in acts of violence. In December 2016, Edgar Maddison Welch entered a pizza restaurant in Washington, DC, and discharged an assault rifle three times (no one was hurt). The restaurant involved had been the subject of online rumours claiming that it was the centre of a human trafficking and child sex ring implausibly led by Hillary Clinton. Beyond the actions of radicalized individuals, fake news is a precursor to and connected with wider, institutionalized violence. In India, false rumours circulating on WhatsApp have triggered lynchings, particularly against Muslim citizens (Banaji, Bhat, Agarwal, Passanha, & Sadhana Pravin, 2019).

Perhaps most worryingly, fake news can become integrated into political projects that seek to capture and harness the coercive power of the state, removing the checks and balances that might normally constrain governments. The Philippines offers a good example of this, where government-related accounts publish fake news stories targeted at regime opponents, which is then followed by mass online trolling of those targets by government supporters, and police intimidation and legal action (Pomerantsev, 2019).

In the aftermath of populist victories around the world, liberal commentators often asked what populist government would look like. After all, the commentators reckoned, the populists had won elections by making half-baked promises that could not possibly be honoured. Now, surely, they would be found out?

In some ways, this prediction was accurate. The sheer ineptitude of some of the populist leaders and those who surrounded them when they assumed office frequently occurred on an epic scale (for an account of the early days of the Trump administration, see Lewis, 2018). Many of the promises made before they won electoral victories were clearly politically impossible – there was not going to be a wall on the US–Mexican border paid for by the Mexican government, nor was there going to be a post-Brexit trade deal with the exact same benefits as EU membership.

At the same time, questioning populists' abilities to fulfil their campaign pledges was hopelessly naive. In the same way as populist political candidates had not played by the norms and rules of liberal democratic politics in their campaigns for office, it was always foolish to expect them to play by the rules when they won.

Specifically, many of the populist leaders elected had no desire to measure their successes in office through the sorts of metrics that would have appealed to the liberal technocrats they had deposed. Ultimately, for at least some of the leaders branded as populist, office holding provided them with access to and control over the coercive power of the state, and the ability to undermine the institutions that they had been challenging rhetorically prior to assuming power. The great risk we are now facing is that fake news becomes just one of the tools in their arsenal for doing this.

Postscript: fake news in the age of COVID-19

In many ways, the emergence of COVID-19 might be seen to have triggered a return to older patterns of media consumption, more reminiscent of the mass communication era. Boris Johnson, for example, did a number of live television broadcasts from Downing Street which were watched by millions as he delivered them. Expertise also appeared to be back in fashion. As well as politicians, government press conferences featured senior advisers. In the UK, the Chief Medical Officer Chris Whitty and Chief Scientific Adviser Sir Patrick Vallance became household names. In the United States, a similar role was filled by Anthony Fauci, the Head of the National Institute of Allergies and Infectious Diseases.

However, in the media environment described in this book, it is unsurprising to learn that COVID-19 also generated fake news. This ranged from the President of the United States suggesting that injecting bleach might be a good way to kill the virus, to theories claiming that 5G internet was the real cause of the outbreak. In the latter case, these rumours even led to vigilante attacks on mobile phone masts. At the time of writing, the very first licensed doses of a COVID-19 vaccine are being administered, which seems likely to increase the attention paid to anti-vaccination movements and conspiracy theories.

Crisis has a propensity to bring existing political tensions into sharper relief (on the role of crisis in politics, see the discussion in Anstead, 2018). It is therefore not surprising that COVID-19 has led to a showdown between technocratic, evidence-based policy-making and more populist political ideas, fuelled by conspiracy theories and mistrust.

It is also possible to argue that the coronavirus crisis has highlighted both the complex nature of truth in science and policy-making, and the simplistic way it is deployed in political rhetoric. Politicians frequently claimed that they were 'following the science' when imposing restrictions on the public, a rhetorical strategy that was an attempt to distance themselves from unpopular decisions. However, it was also very clear that at times the science was uncertain, evolving rapidly and subject to expert disagreement. This was rarely reflected, even in mainstream media coverage.

The COVID-19 pandemic also shaped the context of the 2020 US presidential election, which was lost by Donald Trump. Trump went down as he campaigned and as he governed, spreading falsehoods, this time about election rigging and fraudulent postal voting. It would be very easy to think about the Trump years as an aberration and hope for a return to politics as normal, leaving talk of fake news behind us. This would be a mistake. Plenty of other countries in the world prove that fake news is still a problem. Even more troubling, is that while Trump may be gone, the reasons for his rise still remain. The risk posed by fake news and the brand of politics it is connected with are not going away.

further reading

Recent years have seen a number of books published on the topic of fake news. McNair (2017) offers a wide-ranging discussion on the subject, focused on the intersection between fake news and political communication. McIntyre's (2018) volume on post truth provides interesting insights into some of the cognitive processes surrounding fake news as well as a discussion of the role of postmodernist thought. Farkas and Schou (2019) provide an alternative perspective, arguing that our contemporary fixation on fake news presupposed an idealized and truthful past.

On the American experience of fake news, Benkler et al. (2018) provide an account of the different ways information circulates on the political left and right, while Jamieson (2020) examines Russian involvement in the 2016 election. The same story is well (if rather dryly) told in the final reports of the Mueller inquiry (2019). A wider, more comparative perspective is bought to these issues by Howard (2020). Howard and his collaborators have also produced a number of research reports on similar topics which are freely available on the Oxford Internet Institute website.

Pomerantsev (2019) offers an engaging, very personal and wide-ranging account of fake news in different national contexts. Banaji et al.'s (2019) work on WhatsApp and political violence in India demonstrates the increasing importance of closed messaging services in this area.

The challenges facing contemporary democracy are central to the argument in this book. Recent years have seen a vast number of books published on this topic, but a good starting point is Mounk (2018). Readers looking for a more optimistic take might enjoy reading Runciman (2017), who argues that democracies are regularly in some form of crisis, but they are also very robust.

A good insight into the policy debates surrounding fake news and regulation is offered by the work of the House of Commons Digital, Culture, Media and Sport Committee (2019). The London School of Economics' Truth Trust and Technology Commission (2018) working group produced a detailed report on possible regulatory solutions.

There are a variety of freely available data resources for anyone wanting to explore more about media and news consumption. The UK's media regulator Ofcom regularly publishes reports based on extensive surveys looking at the use of and attitudes to media. Pew Research has undertaken similar work in the United States. The Reuters Institute at Oxford University has gathered a wonderful treasure trove of comparative data in recent years.

references

Achen, C. H., & Bartels, L. M. (2017). *Democracy for realists: Why elections do not produce responsive government*. Princeton, NJ: Princeton University Press.

Allcott, H., & Gentzkow, M. (2017). Social media and fake news in the 2016 election. *Journal of Economic Perspectives, 31*(2), 211–236.

Allen, R. C. (2003). Progress and poverty in early modern Europe. *Economic History Review, 56*(3), 403–443.

Anderson, B. (1983). *Imagined communities: Reflections on the origin and spread of nationalism*. London: Verso.

Anstead, N. (2018). The idea of austerity in British politics, 2003–2013. *Political Studies, 66*(2), 287–305.

Art, D. (2005). *The politics of the Nazi past in Germany and Austria*. Cambridge: Cambridge University Press.

Aston, M. (1980). Lollard women priests. *Journal of Ecclesiastical History, 31*(4), 441–461.

Bakshy, E., Messing, S., & Adamic, L. A. (2015). Exposure to ideologically diverse news and opinion on Facebook. *Science, 348*(6239), 1130–1132.

Banaji, S., Bhat, R., Agarwal, A., Passanha, N., & Sadhana Pravin, M. (2019). WhatsApp vigilantes: An exploration of citizen reception and circulation of WhatsApp misinformation linked to mob violence in India. Retrieved 9 September 2020 from http://eprints.lse.ac.uk/104316

Baudrillard, J. (1995). *The Gulf War did not take place*. Bloomington, IN: Indiana University Press.

BBC News. (2019). Facebook reveals preparations for UK election. Retrieved 10 December 2020 from www.bbc.co.uk/news/technology-50128055

BBC News. (2020). Twitter hides Trump tweet for 'glorifying violence'. Retrieved 30 September 2020 from www.bbc.co.uk/news/technology-52846679

Benkler, Y., Faris, R., & Roberts, H. (2018). *Network propaganda: Manipulation, disinformation, and radicalization in American politics*. Oxford: Oxford University Press.

Berghel, H. (2017). Lies, damn lies, and fake news. *Computer, 50*(2), 80–85.

Bernal, P. (2020). *What do we know and what should we do about internet privacy?* Thousand Oaks, CA: Sage.

Bois, G. (1998). Discussion: On the crisis of the Late Middle Ages. *Medieval History Journal, 1*(2), 311–321.

Bond, S. (2020). Twitter, Facebook Remove Trump Post Over False Claim About Children and COVID-19. Retrieved 30 September 2020 from www.npr.org/2020/08/05/899558311/facebook-removes-trump-post-over-false-claim-about-children-and-covid-19?t=1601470727258

Brewer, M. D. (2005). The rise of partisanship and the expansion of partisan conflict within the American electorate. *Political Research Quarterly, 58*(2), 219–229.

Bruns, A. (2019). Filter bubble. *Internet Policy Review, 8*(4).

Burden, C. (1986). Exposing the Foundations of the Museum. Retrieved 4 December 2020 from www.moca.org/collection/work/exposing-the-foundation-of-the-museum

Buringh, E., & Van Zanden, J. L. (2009). Charting the 'Rise of the West': Manuscripts and printed books in Europe, a long-term perspective from the sixth through eighteenth centuries. *Journal of Economic History, 69*(2), 409–445.

Butler, C. (2002). *Postmodernism: A very short introduction.* Oxford: Oxford University Press.

Chadwick, A. (2007). Digital network repertoires and organizational hybridity. *Political Communication, 24*(3), 283–301.

Collins, B. (2020). *Viral pro-Trump tweets came from fake African American spam accounts, Twitter says.* Retrieved 28 September 2020 from www.nbcnews.com/tech/security/viral-pro-trump-tweets-came-fake-african-american-spam-accounts-n1238553

Crossland, D. (2006). *Did You Hear the One About Hitler?* Retrieved 10 December 2020 from www.spiegel.de/international/new-book-on-nazi-era-humor-did-you-hear-the-one-about-hitler-a-434399.html

Dalton, R. J., & Wattenberg, M. P. (2002). *Parties without partisans: Political change in advanced industrial democracies.* Oxford: Oxford University Press.

Davis, E. (2017). *Post-truth: Why we have reached peak bullshit and what we can do about it.* London: Little, Brown.

de Vreese, C. H. (2007). Context, elites, media and public opinion in referendums: When campaigns really matter. In C. H. de Vreese (Ed.), *The dynamics of referendum campaigns* (pp. 1–20). New York: Springer.

de Vreese, C., Bastos, M., Esser, F., Giglietto, F., Lecheler, S., Pfetsch, B., ... Persily, N. (2019). Public statement from the Co-Chairs and European Advisory

Committee of Social Science One. Retrieved 10 December 2020 from
https://socialscience.one/blog/public-statement-european-advisory-committee-
social-science-one

Dobson, R. B. (1983). *The peasants' revolt of 1381*. New York: Springer.

Doward, J. (2017). How the BBC's truth offensive beat Hitler's propaganda
machine. Retrieved 18 September 2020 from www.theguardian.com/world/
2017/apr/15/bbc-truth-offensive-beat-hitler-propaganda-machine

Druckman, J. N. (2003). The power of television images: The first Kennedy-Nixon
debate revisited. *Journal of Politics*, 65(2), 559–571.

Edmond, C. (2020). 5 charts reveal key racial inequality gaps in the US. Retrieved
28 September 2020 from www.weforum.org/agenda/2020/06/us-race-
economy-education-inequality/

Eisenstein, E. L. (1980). *The printing press as an agent of change*. Cambridge:
Cambridge University Press.

Evans, R. J. (2012). *In defence of history*. London: Granta Publications.

Facebook. (2020). Community Standards 14: Adult nudity and sexual activity.
Retrieved 30 September 2020 from https://en-gb.facebook.com/
communitystandards/adult_nudity_sexual_activity

Farkas, J., & Schou, J. (2019). *Post-truth, fake news and democracy: Mapping
the politics of falsehood*. New York: Routledge.

Finchelstein, F. (2020). *A brief history of fascist lies*. Berkeley, CA: University of
California Press.

Fowler, A., & Hall, A. B. (2018). Do shark attacks influence presidential elections?
Reassessing a prominent finding on voter competence. *Journal of Politics*,
80(4), 1423–1437.

Full Fact. (2017). £350 million EU claim 'a clear misuse of official statistics'.
Retrieved 9 September 2020 from https://fullfact.org/europe/350-million-
week-boris-johnson-statistics-authority-misuse/

Garrett, R. K., Bond, R., & Poulsen, S. (2019). Too many people think satirical
news is real. Retrieved 30 July 2020 from https://theconversation.com/too-
many-people-think-satirical-news-is-real-121666

Given-Wilson, C. (2004). *Chronicles*. London: A&C Black.

Graber, D. A. (1986). Press freedom and the general welfare. *Political Science
Quarterly*, 101(2), 257–275.

Grynbaum, M., & Hsu, T. (2020). Major Networks Cut Away From Trump's
Baseless Fraud Claims. Retrieved 9 December 2020 from www.nytimes.com/
2020/11/05/business/media/trump-tv.html

Guess, A., Nagler, J., & Tucker, J. (2019). Less than you think: Prevalence and predictors of fake news dissemination on Facebook. *Science Advances*, *5*(1), 1–8.

Habermas, J. (1989). *The structural transformation of the public sphere*. London: John Wiley & Sons.

Habgood-Coote, J. (2019). Stop talking about fake news. *Inquiry*, *62*(9–10), 1033–1065.

Hallin, D. C., & Mancini, P. (2004). *Comparing media systems: Three models of media and politics*. Cambridge: Cambridge University Press.

Hamilton, J. M., Coleman, R., Grable, B., & Cole, J. (2006). An enabling environment. *Journalism Studies*, *7*(1), 78–93.

Hanitzsch, T., Van Dalen, A., & Steindl, N. (2018). Caught in the nexus: A comparative and longitudinal analysis of public trust in the press. *International Journal of Press/Politics*, *23*(1), 3–23.

Hirschfeld Davis, J., & Rosenberg, M. (2016). With False Claims, Trump Attacks Media on Turnout and Intelligence Rift. Retrieved 9 December 2020 from www.nytimes.com/2017/01/21/us/politics/trump-white-house-briefing-inauguration-crowd-size.html

Hopp, T., Ferrucci, P., & Vargo, C. J. (2020). Why do people share ideologically extreme, false, and misleading content on social media? A self-report and trace data-based analysis of countermedia content dissemination on Facebook and Twitter. *Human Communication Research*, *46*(4), 357–384.

House of Commons Digital, Culture, Media and Sport Committee. (2019). *Disinformation and 'fake news': Final report*. London: House of Commons.

Howard, P. (2012) Let's Nationalize Facebook. Retrieved 19 January 2021 from https://slate.com/technology/2012/08/facebook-should-be-nationalized-to-protect-user-rights.html

Howard, P. (2020). *Lie machines: How to save democracy from troll armies, deceitful robots, junk news operations, and political operatives*. New Haven, CT: Yale University Press.

Howard, P. N., Ganesh, B., Liotsiou, D., Kelly, J., & François, C. (2019). The IRA, social media and political polarization in the United States, 2012–2018. Retrieved 10 December 2020 from https://digitalcommons.unl.edu/cgi/viewcontent.cgi?article=1004&context=senatedocs

Hughes, C. (2019). It's the EU immigrants stupid! UKIP's core-issue and populist rhetoric on the road to Brexit. *European Journal of Communication*, *34*(3), 248–266.

Hutchinson, A. (2018). Facebook Rolls Out News Feed Algorithm Update to Disincentivize Controversial Content. Retrieved 10 December 2020 from www. socialmediatoday.com/news/facebook-rolls-out-news-feed-algorithm-update-to-disincentivize-controversi/542409/

James, C. (2017). *Clive James on television*. London: Pan Macmillan.

Jamieson, A. (2017). 'You are fake news': Trump attacks CNN and BuzzFeed at press conference. Retrieved from www.theguardian.com/us-news/2017/jan/11/trump-attacks-cnn-buzzfeed-at-press-conference

Jamieson, K. H. (2020). *Cyberwar: How Russian hackers and trolls helped elect a president: What we don't, can't, and do know*. Oxford: Oxford University Press.

Jamieson, K. H., & Cappella, J. N. (2008). *Echo chamber: Rush Limbaugh and the conservative media establishment*. Oxford: Oxford University Press.

Johnson, J. (2020). Cabinet Office to mandate 'digital imprints' on online political ads in disinformation crackdown. Retrieved 9 December 2020 from www.civilserviceworld.com/news/article/cabinet-office-to-mandate-digital-imprints-on-online-political-ads-in-disinformation-crackdown

Jones, J. M. (2018). U.S. Media Trust Continues to Recover From 2016 Low. Retrieved 1 October 2020 from https://news.gallup.com/poll/243665/media-trust-continues-recover-2016-low.aspx

Jones-Jang, S. M., Mortensen, T., & Liu, J. (2019). Does media literacy help identification of fake news? Information literacy helps, but other literacies don't. *American Behavioral Scientist*, 65(2): 371–388

Kaminska, I. (2017). A lesson in fake news from the info-wars of ancient Rome. Retrieved 10 December 2020 from www.ft.com/content/aaf2bb08-dca2-11e6-86ac-f253db7791c6

Kaplan, R. L. (2008). Yellow journalism. In W. Donsbach (Ed.), *The Blackwell international encyclopedia of communication* (pp. 5369–5371). Oxford: Blackwell.

Kessler, G., Rizzo, S., & Kelly, M. (2020). President Trump has made more than 20,000 false or misleading claims. Retrieved 1 October 2020 from www.washingtonpost.com/politics/2020/07/13/president-trump-has-made-more-than-20000-false-or-misleading-claims/

Kim, C. (2020). Poll: 70 percent of Republicans don't think the election was free and fair. Retrieved 9 December 2020 from www.politico.com/news/2020/11/09/republicans-free-fair-elections-435488?nname=politico-nightly&nid=00000170-c000-da87-af78-e185fa700000&nrid=0000014e-f10a-dd93-ad7f-f90f318e0001&nlid=2670445

Krekó, P., & Enyedi, Z. (2018). Orbán's laboratory of illiberalism. *Journal of Democracy, 29*(3), 39–51.

Lai Stirland, S. (2008). Propelled by Internet, Barack Obama Wins Presidency. Retrieved 30 September 2020 from www.wired.com/2008/11/propelled-by-in/

Laura, H. O. (2019). Men and white people believe the news is less reliable now than it was in the past. Women and people of color think it's gotten more reliable. Retrieved 20 January 2019 from www.niemanlab.org/2019/12/ men-and-white-people-believe-the-news-is-less-reliable-now-than-it-was-in-the-past-women-and-people-of-color-think-its-gotten-more-reliable/

Lazarsfeld, P. F., Berelson, B., & Gaudet, H. (1948). *The people's choice.* New York: Columbia University Press.

Lazer, D. M. J., Baum, M. A., Benkler, Y., Berinsky, A. J., Greenhill, K. M., Menczer, F., ... Zittrain, J. L. (2018). The science of fake news. *Science, 359*(6380), 1094–1096.

Lee, T. (2010). Why they don't trust the media: An examination of factors predicting trust. *American Behavioral Scientist, 54*(1), 8–21.

Lewis, M. (2018). *The fifth risk: Undoing democracy.* New York: W.W. Norton.

Lloyd, A. J. (2007). Education, Literacy and the Reading Public. Retrieved 9 December 2020 from www.gale.com/binaries/content/assets/gale-us-en/ primary-sources/intl-gps/intl-gps-essays/full-ghn-contextual-essays/ghn_ essay_bln_lloyd3_website.pdf

Lyotard, J. (1984). *The postmodern condition.* Minneapolis, MN: University of Minnesota Press.

Mair, P. (2013). *Ruling the void: The hollowing of Western democracy.* London: Verso.

Mansfield, M. (2016). How we analysed 70m comments on the Guardian website. Retrieved 22 September 2020 from www.theguardian.com/technology/2016/ apr/12/how-we-analysed-70m-comments-guardian-website

Mason, L. E., Krutka, D., & Stoddard, J. (2018). Media literacy, democracy, and the challenge of fake news. *Journal of Media Literacy Education, 10*(2), 1–10.

McCoy, J., & Somer, M. (2019). Toward a theory of pernicious polarization and how it harms democracies: Comparative evidence and possible remedies. *Annals of the American Academy of Political and Social Science, 681*(1), 234–271.

McCulloh, J. M. (1997). Jewish ritual murder: William of Norwich, Thomas of Monmouth, and the early dissemination of the myth. *Speculum, 72*(3), 698–740.

McHardy, F. (2020). Gossip was a powerful tool for the powerless in ancient Greece. Retrieved 13 August 2020 from https://aeon.co/ideas/gossip-was-a -powerful-tool-for-the-powerless-in-ancient-greece

McIntyre, L. (2018). *Post-truth*. Boston, MA: MIT Press.

McNair, B. (2017). *Fake news: Falsehood, fabrication and fantasy in journalism*. London: Routledge.

Mounk, Y. (2018). *The people vs. democracy: Why our freedom is in danger and how to save it*. Boston, MA: Harvard University Press.

Mueller, R. (2019). *Report on the investigation into Russian interference in the 2016 presidential election*. Washington, DC: US Department of Justice.

Nye, J. S. (2008). Public diplomacy and soft power. *Annals of the American Academy of Political and Social Science, 616*(1), 94–109.

O'Connor, C., & Weatherall, J. O. (2019). *The misinformation age: How false beliefs spread*. New Haven, CT: Yale University Press.

Ofcom. (2019). Ofcom Fines RT £200,000. Retrieved 21 September 2020 from www.ofcom.org.uk/about-ofcom/latest/media/media-releases/2019/ofcom-fines-rt

Ofcom. (2020). News consumption in the UK. Retrieved 1 October 2020 from www.ofcom.org.uk/research-and-data/tv-radio-and-on-demand/news-media/news-consumption

O'Hear, A. (2020). D'ou parles-tu? The post-truth world. Retrieved 8 September 2020 from https://standpointmag.co.uk/issues/august-september-2020/dou-parles-tu-the-post-truth-world/

Pariser, E. (2011). *The filter bubble: What the Internet is hiding from you*. London: Penguin.

Paul, K. (2019). Naked protesters condemn nipple censorship at Facebook headquarters. Retrieved 30 September 2020 from www.theguardian.com/technology/2019/jun/03/facebook-nude-nipple-protest-wethenipple

Perrigo, B. (2019). Boris Johnson's Conservatives Rebranded a Party Twitter Account as 'factcheckUK.' Twitter Wasn't Happy. Retrieved 3 December 2019 from https://time.com/5733786/conservative-fact-check-twitter/

Pomerantsev, P. (2019). *This is not propaganda*. London: Faber & Faber.

Porter, E., Wood, T. J., & Kirby, D. (2018). Sex trafficking, Russian infiltration, birth certificates, and pedophilia: A survey experiment correcting fake news. *Journal of Experimental Political Science, 5*(2), 159–164.

Postman, N. (1985). *Amusing ourselves to death: Public discourse in the age of show business*. London: Penguin.

Pressman, M. (2013). The Myth of FDR's Secret Disability. Retrieved 23 September 2020 from https://ideas.time.com/2013/07/12/the-myth-of-fdrs-secret-disability/

Reuters Institute. (2020). Country and Market Data. Retrieved 21 September 2020 from www.digitalnewsreport.org/survey/2020/country-and-market-data-2020/

Rex, R. (2002). *The Lollards*. New York: Macmillan.

Robinson, M. J. (1976). Public affairs television and the growth of political malaise: The case of 'The Selling of the Pentagon'. *American Political Science Review, 70*(2), 409–432.

Rose, E. M. (2015). *The murder of William of Norwich: The origins of the blood libel in Medieval Europe*. Oxford: Oxford University Press.

Ross, A. (1996). *Science wars* (46). Durham, NC: Duke University Press.

Runciman, D. (2017). *The confidence trap: A history of democracy in crisis from World War I to the present* (rev. ed). Princeton, NJ: Princeton University Press.

Rushe, D. (2018). Zuckerberg's testimony: CEO will defend Facebook as a 'positive force'. Retrieved 30 September 2020 from www.theguardian.com/us-news/2018/apr/09/mark-zuckerberg-facebook-testimony-congress

Schattschneider, E. E. (1960). *Party government*. Piscataway, NJ: Transaction.

Schmidt, V. A. (2010). Taking ideas and discourse seriously: Explaining change through discursive institutionalism as the fourth 'new institutionalism'. *European Political Science Review, 2*(1), 1–25.

Schudson, M. (2001). The objectivity norm in American journalism. *Journalism, 2*, 149–170.

Schudson, M. (2002). The news media as political institutions. *Annual Review of Political Science, 5*(1), 249–269.

Seib, P. (2008). *The Al Jazeera effect: How the new global media are reshaping world politics*. Lincoln, NE: Potomac Books.

Shipman, T. (2016). *All out war: The full story of how Brexit sank Britain's political class*. London: HarperCollins.

Silverman, C. (2016a). How Teens In The Balkans Are Duping Trump Supporters With Fake News. Retrieved 3 August 2020 from www.buzzfeednews.com/article/craigsilverman/how-macedonia-became-a-global-hub-for-pro-trump-misinfo

Silverman, C. (2016b). This Analysis Shows How Viral Fake Election News Stories Outperformed Real News On Facebook. Retrieved 28 September from www.buzzfeednews.com/article/craigsilverman/viral-fake-election-news-outperformed-real-news-on-facebook#.bp90yKJ1W

Smith, A. (2020). Amazon Stops Telling People What They Have Bought in Emails. Retrieved 28 September 2020 from www.independent.co.uk/life-style/gadgets-and-tech/news/amazon-order-email-confirmation-shipping-details-a9543966.html

Snyder, T. (2017). *On tyranny*. New York: Random House.

Statistica. (2020). The 100 largest companies in the world by market capitalization in 2020. Retrieved 10 December 2020 from www.statista.com/statistics/263264/top-companies-in-the-world-by-market-capitalization/

Stencil, M., & Luther, J. (2019). Reporters' Lab fact checking tally tops 200. Retrieved 9 September 2020 from https://reporterslab.org/reporters-lab-fact-checking-tally-tops-200/

Strömbäck, J., Djerf-Pierre, M., & Shehata, A. (2013). The dynamics of political interest and news media consumption: A longitudinal perspective. *International Journal of Public Opinion Research, 25*(4), 414–435.

Sunstein, C. R. (2001). *Republic.com*. Princeton, NJ: Princeton University Press.

Tandoc, E. C., Lim, Z. W., & Ling, R. (2018). Defining 'Fake News'. *Digital Journalism, 6*(2), 137–153.

Taunton, W. (2014). Print Culture. Retrieved 17 September 2020 from www.bl.uk/romantics-and-victorians/articles/print-culture

Thomasson, E. (2018). Germany looks to revise social media law as Europe watches. Retrieved 9 September 2020 from www.reuters.com/article/us-germany-hatespeech/germany-looks-to-revise-social-media-law-as-europe-watches-idUSKCN1GK1BN

Truth Trust and Technology Commission. (2018). *Tackling the information crisis: A policy framework for media system resilience*. London: Department of Media and Communications, London School of Economics.

Van Duyn, E., & Collier, J. (2019). Priming and fake news: The effects of elite discourse on evaluations of news media. *Mass Communication and Society, 22*(1), 29–48.

Vancil, D. L., & Pendell, S. D. (1987). *The myth of viewer-listener disagreement in the first Kennedy-Nixon debate. 38*(1), 16–27.

Waisbord, S. (2018). Truth is what happens to news: On journalism, fake news, and post-truth. *Journalism Studies, 19*(13), 1866–1878.

Walter, N., Cohen, J., Holbert, R. L., & Morag, Y. (2019). Fact-checking: A meta-analysis of what works and for whom. *Political Communication, 37*(3), 1–26.

Wardle, C., & Derakhshan, H. (2017). *Information disorder: Toward an interdisciplinary framework for research and policy making* (27). Strasbourg: Council of Europe.

Wilkerson, M. M. (1932). *Public opinion and the Spanish-American War*. Baton Rouge, LA: Louisiana State University Press.

Young, D. G., & Tisinger, R. M. (2006). Dispelling late-night myths: News consumption among late-night comedy viewers and the predictors of exposure to various late-night shows. *Harvard International Journal of Press/Politics, 11*(3), 113–134.

Zelizer, B. (1992). CNN, the Gulf War, and journalistic practice. *Journal of Communication, 42*(1), 66–81.

Ziegler, P. (2013). *The Black Death*. London: Faber & Faber.

Zuckerman, L. (2004). *The rape of Belgium: The untold story of World War I*. New York and London: NYU Press.

index